GRIEF IS FOR PEOPLE

Also by Sloane Crosley

FICTION

Cult Classic
The Clasp

NONFICTION

Look Alive Out There
How Did You Get This Number
I Was Told There'd Be Cake

GRIEF
IS
FOR
PEOPLE

SLOANE CROSLEY

MCD ◯ FARRAR, STRAUS AND GIROUX NEW YORK

MCD
Farrar, Straus and Giroux
120 Broadway, New York 10271

Grateful acknowledgment is made for permission to reprint lines from "Moments in the Woods," from *Into the Woods*. Words and Music by Stephen Sondheim © 1988 RILTING MUSIC, INC. All Rights Administered by WC MUSIC CORP. All Rights Reserved. Used by Permission. Reprinted by Permission of Hal Leonard LLC.

ISBN 9780374609849

Designed by Abby Kagan

This is a work of nonfiction. However, some timelines and identifying characteristics have been altered to protect the privacy of a few individuals, and the dialogue has been reconstructed to the best of the author's recollection.

For Russell Perreault

Oh, if life were made of moments,
Even now and then a bad one—!
But if life were only moments,
Then you'd never know you had one.

—STEPHEN SONDHEIM, *Into the Woods*

Either you jump out the window or you live.

—BROOKE HAYWARD, *Haywire*

CONTENTS

PART I
DON'T LET ME
KEEP YOU

(DENIAL)

All burglaries are alike, but every burglary is uninsured in its own way. On June 27, 2019, at 5:15 p.m., I leave my apartment for one hour and come home to find all my jewelry missing. This is the front entrance of the story, the facts of the case. Container first, emotion second. As if by offering up an order of events, the significance of those events will fill itself in automatically. But that story ends before it begins, without ever *really* being told. The thief enters the story through my bedroom window. He scurries up the corroded metal steps of my fire escape. He lifts the screen, then the glass, crouching to make himself small. Into the stillness of my bedroom come his dirty boots, sinking into the white comforter. To be fair, he has no choice but to step on the comforter.

The bed is flush with the window because it takes up half the room.

Once inside, the thief takes a total of five minutes and forty-one pieces of jewelry. Amid the otherwise unremarkable loot are my grandmother's amber amulet, the size of an apricot, as well as her green cocktail ring, a dome with tiers of tourmaline (think kryptonite, think dish soap).

But let us pause here, before you get too turned around.

My grandmother was an awful person. I've never met anyone who misses her. She was abusive and creative about it. If she was irritated at one of her children, she would instruct the other two to give the offending child the silent treatment. When my mother was a kid, she would be sent to her room with the understanding that my grandmother would be up at any minute with a belt. Sometimes she showed. Sometimes she didn't. Sometimes she'd dig her nails into my mother's arm until the skin broke, an act of violence exacerbated by the bafflement that followed: *Darling, whatever have you done to yourself?* By the time this woman and I overlapped in sentience and height, she was cordial enough. Hinged enough. Still, the longest conversation I had with her was on the day of my college graduation. She swanned into town, chucked a pearl bracelet across a restaurant table, and offered to pay for graduate school. She rescinded the offer after I mailed my applications. I don't know why. The bracelet I got to keep.

Well, for a while, anyway.

My efforts to repurpose her objects, to give them the soul they never had, have been slower than their financial appreciation. The necklace originally belonged to my great-grandmother, and apparently she was no picnic either. I have long suspected these objects of not wanting to be on me, the green ring sensing an unfamiliar pulse pass through it. My mother, the least favored child, was relegated to the footnotes of the will, so these items are my sole inheritance. But I have thought of them as cursed. I've never worn them on planes. And now a stranger is in my home, packing up the remnants of a cruel woman and carting them off. Unfortunately, they are worth quite a bit of money; even I do not know how much. I've never had them appraised, which would've been necessary to get them insured. Maybe because appraisal always seemed too adult, like hiring a lawyer or buying a Waterpik. Maybe because I have felt about these things the way I felt about my grandmother, that it was not my job to look after them but their job to look after me.

The thief also steals my other grandmother's silver engagement band, a charm bracelet built for smaller wrists, and a cow-shaped pin I found on the street in Madison, Wisconsin. All I have been left and all I would leave are being dumped into a stranger's backpack.

It's indulgent to tell the story like this, in the present tense. As if I can still stop it. As if there's an ankle to be grabbed. There's no ankle. I can't stop what's already happened. But this is the only way I can explain the events of June 27, 2019, or the days that follow it. Thirty days, down to the hour, that will be bookended by personal loss. Thirty days, down to the hour, that I cannot know will be a precursor to a year of global loss. Eventually, I will look back on the burglary and see it for what it is, a dark gift of delineation. I know when my first bomb went off. Not everyone gets to know.

And no one is obliged to learn something from loss. This is a horrible thing we do to the newly stricken, encouraging them to remember the good times while they're still in the fetal position. Like feeding steak to a baby. I have read the grief literature and the grief philosophy and, God help me, listened to the grief podcasts, and the most practical thing I have learned is the power of the present tense. The past is quicksand and the future is unknowable, but in the present, you get to float. Nothing is missing, nothing is hypothetical.

In truth, I am writing these words on the evening of August 27, 2019. It's a Tuesday. The Amazon is on fire.

It's been two months since the burglary.

It's been one month since the violent death of my dearest friend.

This occurred on the evening of July 27, 2019.

I will be editing these sentences much later, after several dozen 27ths have passed, when the gap between the past and the present is more of a chasm. By then, I will be able to better control how I think of these absences. I will be able to proceed with a conversation without flinching when someone mentions the wrong movie or the wrong song. But right now, I am in denial that my friend is gone. I am, despite overwhelming evidence to the contrary, in denial that the jewelry is gone.

Human beings are the only animals that experience denial. All creatures will try to survive under attack, will burrow when under siege or limp through the forest. But they recognize trouble when it hits. Not one fish in the history of fish, having gotten its fins chewed off, needs another fish's perspective: *I don't know, Tom, that looks pretty bad.* Denial is humankind's specialty, our handy aversion. We are so allergic to our own mortality; we'll do anything to make it not so. Denial is also the weirdest stage of grief because it so closely mimics stupidity. But it can't be helped. I can't be helped. I am holding these losses as an aunt might, as if they are familiar but not quite mine. As if they are books I will be allowed to return to some centralized sadness library.

In the days immediately following the burglary, I am a tragic figure among my friends but in a fun way. Something real has happened to me. But not to my body. I am not raped or maimed or consigned to a fatal disease. I'll live. Plus, I come bearing a mystery, one that surely can be solved, right here, right now, over this shared appetizer. Amateur detectives, each friend is more convinced than the last that *she* will be the one to solve my case. The burglary is a brainteaser, a proposition shot up from a pistol. We had a book like this in our house growing up, a pop-philosophy bestseller called *The Book of Questions*. The only question I remember verbatim is this one:

You and someone you love deeply are placed in separate rooms, each with a button next to you. You each know that you both will be killed unless one of you presses your button in the next 60 minutes. You also know that the first to hit the button will save the other, but immediately die. What would you do?

Even if you give an answer that will absolutely result in divorce, the wording prevents you from being too cocky about murder. What *would* you do? Not what *do* you do. In this same way, people are drawn to the thought experiment of the burglary more than the burglary itself. Some point out that I have been the victim of a retro crime. Yes, I'm aware that the 1970s came back to kick me in the face. Out of kindness or curiosity, they demand a tour of the story. But they aren't having fun on the tour. They adopt the expressions of nurses, exchanging furtive glances about the drip. Fine then, tell me what to do. They advise me to do nothing, to write nothing, only to get some sleep and install an alarm system. They mean well. But what they do not understand is that if I do not capture what I have lost, it will be like losing it twice.

At first, I insist there is no trauma. As a New Yorker, my threshold for a scarring experience involves being knocked unconscious and shoved into a barrel. I wasn't even home for this. But the trauma humps my leg like a dog. I pick at memory scabs, recalling the sound of the amber amulet sputtering along its chain. On the subway, I stare at other people's jewelry, necklaces on fleshy display stands. I run my thumb over the base of my pinkie as if, if I push hard enough, a ring will pop out.

Am I too attached to these objects? Is this an ignoble level of attachment for a grown woman to have?

One hour. One lousy hour.

I'd gone to get a hand X-ray nearby, thus leaving behind the silver rings I wore every day for twenty years. And what is there to be said about this? *Luck* is a dirty word when you're out of it. There is no sign of forced entry when I return, though this is not something I generally scan for upon entering my apartment. But then I spot several of the ceramic drawers where I keep my jewelry, smashed on the bedroom floor. My first thought is: *Earthquake?* The cat has aged out of mayhem. Then I notice the rest of the drawers, turned over on the bed, and follow the trail to the open window. Most traumatic events present their size and shape fairly quickly. But some unfurl slowly, like a fist loosening its grip. When I call 911, my voice is urgent but searching. It's the voice of someone who has run onto a train as the doors are shutting. *Is this the express? Have I gotten on the express?* It has never before occurred to me that 911 operators must hear an eerie amount of calm, of people seeking confirmation that they should be calling at all. The operator is in the midst of sharing a joke with her colleague when she picks up. She can't quite pull it together in time. She says: "Nine-ha-ha-one-one, what's your emergency?"

My friend Russell, who is dead now, enters the story before it begins. In a way, the thief is stealing from him too. He was here first. The smashed ceramic drawers belong to a 1920s Dutch spice cabinet we bought together, along the grassy aisles of a flea market in Connecticut. This was fifteen years ago, back when I still worked in book publishing, back when Russell was still my boss, a moniker I kept using long after he stopped being allowed to tell me what to do. He wasn't so fond of it when it applied. *You know,* he'd say, wounded, *I introduce you to people as my friend.* The fact that one of us could fire the other was immaterial. Our job titles, Executive Director of Publicity and Associate Director of Publicity, were meaningless strings of code.

The price of weekend visits to the house he shared with his

partner was a 6:00 a.m. wake-up call to drive to the edge of a field and drink instant coffee from foam cups. His partner and I would groggily plod along as Russell zipped between blankets pinned down by cheap trinkets: cracked colanders, down-on-their-luck bunnies, cloudy prohibition bottles, pillows crocheted with "If you lived here, you'd be home by now."

A flea market is the perfect intersection of frugality and taste, and no one knew that better than Russell. No bazaar has seen a haggler like him—the impish smile of a child, the timeless charm of a movie star, the competitive edge of a Spartan. See that open face, like a doll's, those gray-blue eyes, that thatch of salt-and-pepper hair, seemingly scalped from the roof of an English country house. It feels ludicrous to go on here, to launch into a description of this person I loved so much. A rare instance in which less information would make life easier. The narrowing of traits is a necessary betrayal of the dead, but one must tread carefully in situations like these. Once, I was asked to blurb the memoir of a woman whose mother had died, but the more the book told me to think of her as the best of all mothers, the less I could follow instructions. I felt for the author, for the fact that this precious relationship was in the hands of someone unmoved by the details. But this is what comes of writing not "I miss this person," but "Miss this person as I do." It's too much laundering of empathy.

So, for now, in place of further description of Russell, I will ask only that you turn your attention to the time *Martha Stewart Living* offered to photograph his collection of mid-century earthenware water jugs. He refused. He feared he'd never know the joy of fleecing an unsuspecting vendor again.

"Just look at what they did to milk glass."

Russell spotted the spice cabinet first. He dragged me by my sleeve to come see it, suggesting I could store jewelry inside. But in a land of five-dollar items, the cabinet cost more than a hundred dollars. I was embarrassed that I couldn't get the seller to budge, so I bought some Girl Scout patches instead, featuring girls doing wholesome things. Like splitting logs. Russell insisted that if the cabinet was still there on our way out, I had to get it. He would drive it into the city himself.

"Told you," he said, helping the seller wrap it up. "It was waiting for you."

This is not your typical spice cabinet. It's a massive item, three feet wide with a solid wooden frame into which slide fourteen white drawers, painted with green trim. It was manufactured in Holland, so the drawers are labeled in Dutch. Small ones are for *peper* and *saffraan*, large ones are for *suiker* and *thee*. In the center is a ceramic door with a pewter knob. The door is labeled *eieren*. I'd say I don't know on what planet eggs qualify as a spice, but I do know: the Netherlands. Behind the egg door are two thin wooden shelves with six holes each. They are ideal for dangling necklaces.

When the thief opens the egg door, he grabs the shelves as one might grab a bowling ball. Or as if one were an unusually aggressive beekeeper. He yanks them so roughly from their tracks, a gold chain gets caught and snaps in two.

While I wait for the police to come, I call Russell to confess what happened. He is my favorite person, the one who somehow sees me both as I want to be seen and as I actually am, the one whose belief in me over the years has been the most earned (he is not my parent), the most pure (he is not my boyfriend), and the most forgiving (he is my friend). There are, of course, days when he is not my favorite person, days when I would pay him to be a little less like himself. But my instinct to tell him everything and immediately, to empty my pockets of stories for him, has always been strong. It's an odd sensation, to be an adult and look up to another adult. Not just to hold him in high regard, but to adopt his tastes and feel a sense of flattery when he adopts yours. The reason I was hesitant to demonstrate my poor haggling skills in front of Russell was because I wanted there to be no division between us. I wanted us to be the same, always.

Calling him really does feel like a confession, like I should've protected what I had while I still had it. It's harder to tell Russell about the burglary than it will be to tell my own mother, a direct descendant of the bracelet-tossing child tormentor. My mother will be distracted by the matter of my personal safety. But Russell understands objects as spiritual avatars, more loyal than most, more tolerable than any. Which is why his reaction surprises me.

He adores tales of my wicked and miserly grandmother, of her Joan Crawford *joie de vivre*, and is saddened that their physical prompts have been taken away, but he is *unmoored* by the missing egg shelves. He dwells on their removal, as if this action is from the wrong heist movie. When I remind him of the actual jewelry that was taken—of the chain that snapped in two, of the rings he's mindlessly turned over in his palm during talks on his porch—he steers the conversation back to the shelves. *It's just so unnecessary.* Their absence from the cabinet has not added insult to injury; their absence is the injury. It will be a long time before

I realize this is because Russell cannot stomach the sadness of the larger violation. He cannot stomach sadness period.

Two cops arrive. These are the responding officers. I lean on my doorframe as they clonk up the stairs, asking me how I am. I tell them "not awesome" and invite them in with a sweep of my arm.

"All right," says the first cop, "give us the tour."

I walk them into the bedroom, where, as a group, we come to the conclusion that there's a window in here. Then we file back into the main room, where the second cop informs me that my laptop is on the table. Three more cops show up, including one with a fingerprint kit. She has an air of competence about her. When she requests permission to dust, I wonder under what circumstances I would not want that.

"It makes a mess," she explains. "You seem like a neat person."

Normally, I would accept this as a compliment but I have already begun searching for clues as to how I could have brought this on. I have already begun wondering how much the external assessment of me as a person in the world, one who has enough material goods to require a cabinet, might have factored into this crime. This notion, that this is not a crime of convenience but one of calculation, is dangerous. I can sense it licking its lips in the corner. I get a lot of packages. That the packages contain books or galleys of books is not something I can explain to a criminal mastermind retroactively. I live in the West Village, in a mediocre building surrounded by extravagant fortresses. I can't pay rent in this neighborhood and have nothing, though I can have nothing because I pay rent here. It's a conundrum. But perhaps no factor is so outlandish as the fact that, four years ago, I published a whole novel about stolen jewelry.

Our hero breaks into a French château to steal a necklace. He does this by scaling a wall and climbing through a bedroom window.

Did the novel do this? Rather, are there enough copies of the novel in circulation to do this? This line of concern is born from an unholy mixture of ego and paranoia. I wouldn't entertain it were it not for one minor detail: All my jewelry is missing.

As the cops ask me questions, staticky voices coming from their hips, my thoughts enter the seventh circle of sexism. Clearly this happened because I am a woman, trapped in a perfect storm of profession and age. I hail from a generation that beefed up résumés and deployed adverbs. We had to make ourselves appealing before the dawn of social media, when there was no daily pastiche of the self and therefore less space for self-deprecation. If you got anyone's attention, you combed your hair and put your pants on. You made it count. As adults, women such as myself are caught in the messaging middle, after those who dressed up for planes, before those who dressed down for dates. Perhaps I have not done such a bang-up job as I thought, straddling the line between the Show-Off generation and the Whatever one.

Still, the idea that I have been punished for the dubiously impactful enterprise that is *book promotion* makes me want to punch a hole through the wall. I think of the older book critic who once crossed a party to chastise me for posting photos of myself on Instagram. Self-appointed custodian of that platform's purity, the book critic decided: "Pictures should be of what you see, not of what the world sees when it sees you."

"Do you have any enemies?" asks one of the cops, corralling my attention.

"Sorry, what?"

"Enemies."

"Nemeses?"

"No, enemies."

"Ah."

I can see the forensics cop in my bedroom, unpacking her kit, adding objects to the room. Her job is so different from the thief's. I make my way over to her and share my book promotion theory. When the novel came out, I explain, I wrote an article for a fashion magazine about the relationship between jewelry and sentimentality. She nods. She is feather-dusting a pile of paperbacks.

"There were photographs," I say, as if she has spontaneously forgotten what we're talking about, "in the magazine."

"Of this apartment?"

"No, of an old one."

"Maybe the thief reads that magazine."

I scoff, dismissing my own theory upon hearing it echoed back to me.

"Well, certainly not back issues."

She snorts. I snort. We're having fun, aren't we? Considering?

At long last, a muscular detective arrives, squeezing past his colleagues. He's wearing a purple tie and a gray suit that pulls at the armpits. He attempts to jog my short-term memory: Have I had anyone working in my apartment? A handyman? A housekeeper? I shake my head. A houseguest? A party? The only recent visitor is the man I broke up with one week prior.

Pencils down. Here is the whiff of an inside job, of less paperwork. I now must inform the room that this man didn't exactly fight for our relationship. He wouldn't recognize a piece of my jewelry if he swallowed it. Furthermore, he's a creative director who paints on the weekends, and not like Francis Bacon. He's not in touch with a criminal element. Still, I amuse myself, imagining what would happen if I let the police think this person was heartbroken enough for retaliation. I picture them searching his house, finding the axe he keeps nailed to a wall, not understanding this is a weapon only insofar as hipster affectation is a weapon.

"Maybe he cared more than you thought," suggests one of the cops.

"No, he cared exactly as much as I thought."

I'd been working for Russell for five years, in the publicity department at Vintage Books, the paperback arm of the fabled Knopf, when I stumbled upon my own résumé in the back of a filing cabinet. He must've been seeing a lot of candidates for my job, because he'd scribbled in the margins: *Long brown hair. Square ring.* I felt both chuffed and threatened by the other résumés pressed against mine—was there a world in which he thought we might not work out? On my pointer finger I wore the same ring, a square of tiger's eye framed in silver, that he complimented the day he interviewed me.

Before I met Russell, I'd been employed by a more commercial publishing house, where my fellow assistants were in book publicity because they got lost on their way to corporate publicity or because they got lost on their way to academia. During my time there, one got promoted, one got fired, one left for graduate school, and two went to do PR for actual oil companies. But we were all victims of the same gnarly paper cuts from the same glossy author photos. We filled out the same overtime forms under the same recessed lighting and drank the same bomb-shelter coffee from the same mugs. And we were friends. Which is why, even after Russell offered me the job at Vintage, I was hesitant to jump ship. What if I didn't like these new people as much? I asked to come in for a second interview.

It takes a special brand of brat to do what I did. I was twenty-five and proficient in nothing. But Russell allowed me to return to his office, where I unleashed a barrage of questions, all of which he gamely answered. When I was through, he exhaled in a way that seemed like a prelude to a dismissal. Plenty of people would take this job without even knowing to whom they'd be reporting. I was not yet familiar with the trajectory of Russell's career, but I could sense the scope of it just by sitting across from him. His rolodex was open to the "C" tab. Caro, Robert. I later learned that, with the exception of a stint at Oxford University Press ("my walkabout," as he called it), he had been with the company since 1990.

Russell put his elbows on his desk, leaned forward, and, with the greatest restraint he could muster, asked me what the hell I thought I was doing.

"Sorry?"

"Seriously," he said, "what are you doing? It's like you've been admitted to Harvard but first you need a tour of the bathrooms."

At the turn of the century, Knopf was the most sought-after publishing house in America, both to be published by and to work for. The number of houses from which a "big" book could spring felt limited, and here, under one venerated roof, was the marketing budget of a small country, the first printings in the six-figures, and the brains of a couple dozen Nobel Prize winners. When a writer signed a book deal with Knopf, it was like a minor knighting. When a prestigious author turned out to already be published there, it was: *Of course.* Vintage was the paperback arm of it all, a dedicated department where those books lived on in perpetuity. It was an archive befitting the dead and a garden befitting the living. Home of classics, home of second chances. And Russell ran it. He had drunk the Kool-Aid. He had also mixed the Kool-Aid.

He instructed me to go over to his shelves, close my eyes, and pick a book. I was to go home that night, read it, and if I didn't see the value in it, I didn't have to work for him. His tone was casual but I could hear the worry behind it. He was twelve years older, thirty-seven, the age at which you start realizing that you only get so many loves of your life. But I was too young to start mourning connections the moment I made them.

I chose *Heartburn* by Nora Ephron.

Over the next decade, Russell delighted in telling people I was "working as a waitress in a cocktail bar" when he hired me. He had issued a course correction that would be imperceptible to the naked eye—I stopped commuting to one publishing house and started commuting to another, even the coffee was the same—but he knew better. Find one of us, pull the string, you'd find the other. Ours was the kind of partnership that felt transferable. Give us a designer's discount and we will decorate your house. Give us some forceps and we will deliver your baby. Give us adjoining desks and we will crack your case. We moved fluidly among the roles of parent, child, sibling, and subordinate, swapping positions as they do in experimental theater.

The first time I published a piece of my own writing, an essay in *The Village Voice*, I thought I might have to avoid mentioning it at work. Or at least put its existence down as a fluke. The essay must have tripped and fallen into an editor's in-box. Media was more siloed then and one's side ambitions did not make one *more* employable.

Russell papered the hallway with copies of the essay. He slid a few underneath occupied bathroom stalls.

This is someone who played tricks with equal enthusiasm. A puckish breeze blowing through the self-serious trees, he served as office mascot. He'd rearrange the objects on people's desks to see if they noticed or leave joke presents in our mailboxes. He'd cut out advertisements for medical creams and vacation packages to Siberia and tape them to our monitors. He set up a fake e-mail account from my cat, from which I'd receive missives like "Mommy, how come you didn't come home last night?" or "Mommy, how come you're wearing the same outfit two days in a row?"

One afternoon, after we'd had lunch with an author I admired, I came back to my desk to find an e-mail from Russell: *See below. Let's discuss.* I scrolled down:

Dear Russell: What a pleasure it was to meet with you and Sloane today. Please don't say anything, but she seems a bit young to be handling my publicity campaign. Is there a way you can oversee her more closely?

I felt a hollowness expand in my chest as I tried to take in the lines. Russell appeared in my doorframe.

"How should I respond?" he asked, unable to control his snickering.

I took a closer look at the e-mail address, which was too obvious to be real. There was also a typo in the time stamp.

"You're an asshole."

It dawned on us both that I could forward the e-mail to Human Resources. Russell dove for the delete key. I tried to block him, but he won, knocking over a full bottle of soda in the process. As we caught our breath, watching the soda drip over the cliff of my desk and onto a power strip, we realized the *sent* version of the e-mail was still on his computer. He darted down the hall. I ran after him, lunging and grabbing his ankle, and we both went flying onto the unforgiving office carpeting. I scraped my elbow. The tiger's-eye ring scratched his cheek.

"*Children,*" our boss greeted us as he passed, stepping over our prostrate bodies.

But like I said: There are no ankles left to be grabbed. It's impossible to predict how much you'll miss something when it's gone, to game grief in advance. We fend off the worry that we're taking our lives for granted by feeding ourselves the lie that we understand the value of their components. This belief is necessary for our choices, for the ordering of priorities. But it's flimsy. You can play the game of identifying what you'd save in a fire all you want, but you will only ever be mostly right. I have a decent read on how much Russell means to me, having spent more hours of my adult life with this man than any other, but it does not occur to me that I am this attached to the jewelry until I start cataloging it for the police report.

A city of trinkets rises in my mind. Like any skyline, there are iconic sections, but there are also surprises that appear as I round each corner: a turquoise pin from a college friend, a beaded necklace from my niece, a pearl I dug out of the ocean with my own hands. I curse as I write their names.

"Fuck," I say, "I guess I need better window locks."

"Yeah," says one of the cops, "that and a swear jar."

Where this New York City police officer parked his turnip truck, I do not know, but I try to channel those Girl Scouts on their patches, those upstanding citizens. Alas, the patches are gone. They were in the motherfucking cabinet.

"You know what?" I say. "Welcome to New York. You get broken into and people curse here. Everybody gets to learn a lesson."

I clap as I say it: Everybody. Gets. To. Learn. A. Lesson.

After I have my fingerprints taken, I escort everyone out the door. As I close it, I leave smudges on the brass doorknob. Fingerprints don't disintegrate, and mine are all over this apartment, in various states of clarity. Perhaps the thief's are here now too. Somehow this is not as upsetting as the idea of my fingerprints *outside* the apartment, on the move, oily stowaways on stolen surfaces. Still, I'm glad to be alone. The robbery is gestating, maximizing and minimizing with each breath. I need silence so I can listen to it, so that I can understand its size. It's emitting a steady moan that I do not yet understand is also about Russell. His cabinet. His taste. His bright idea. His satisfaction as he loaded it into the car. His prints mingled with mine.

I am up half the night cleaning fingerprint dust, which is, ironically, a lot like mopping up blood. You swirl carbon in circles until, four or five paper towel wads in, it agrees to come with you. Before bed, I scrub under my nails, but the pads of my feet will stay black for weeks. Weeks during which I will stand in front of the cabinet the way the cat stands in front of her automated feeder, as if trying to will its contents into the bowl. I touch my temple to the wooden frame. I am waiting for the things I love to come back to me, to tell me they were only joking.

Russell had zero facility for office politics. He was an excellent mentor so long as you didn't expect anything resembling patience. He kept a quote, attributed to Louis XIV, pinned above his desk: "I have been almost obligated to wait." This sort of blunt managerial style was not only tolerated but protected in book editors, who spent years crafting interpersonal gauntlets, doling out eye contact like a finite resource. Not so for publicists. We were hired to interact, to nudge, to smooth out the edges of any conversation. Shortly after I left Vintage to write full-time, I had an idea for a TV pilot, a comedy that would take place in the Human Resources department of a publishing house. Because I'd worked in the building and knew its personalities, the HR director agreed to share some "generally colorful" stories. No names, he emphasized in advance, and no guesses at names. Though he did ask me to produce one of my own: To whom had I reported, again?

"Oh, *well*," he said, "you could do a whole spin-off about that one."

In his own defense, Russell loved to tell a self-styled fable from before my time, about the woman who came to him for an informational interview. She was organized and well-read and couldn't understand why no one would hire her. Russell leaped at the chance to explain.

"First of all," he said, "you asked me where my office was and it's in the signature of my e-mail. So you just told me you'd make more work for me. Second of all, you're not fun. This is a seven-person department. I have to live with you."

I could just see him scribbling in the margins of her résumé: *Not fun.*

Years later, when the woman became a successful newspaper editor, she wrote Russell a handwritten note, thanking him for this life-changing candor. He pinned it above his desk too. Sometimes he'd wordlessly point, as if to say, "Talk to the note."

"Uh-huh," I'd say. "That's one person."

Russell was frank with those who reported to him because he expected them to be frank in return, to tell him when an author was unhappy, to edit the corny jokes out of his pitch letters, to chastise him for being late to a meeting. So many of us will accept adoration even if it's not about us, even if it's only about the perception of us. Or some service we provide. We are happy to be cast in other people's plays so long as we're given a role. But Russell was adamant that he be adored for exactly who he was. Perhaps it had something to do with spending the first half of his life trying to blend into a world in which he could never fully be himself, where repression was the price of acceptance. Either way, Russell liked to say that after being loved, being *adored* is the best experience there is.

And once you established that you did, in fact, adore him, you had to maintain. It was like throwing a ball at a puppy. He'd send me a text and then appear in my office door, asking me if I'd read the text.

"Go away."

"Are you annoyed at me?"

"Yes."

"Are you in a bad mood?"

"I am now."

But the second he sulked down the hall, I'd roll my chair after him, pleading for him to come back. Come back, come back. Please come back.

And then it was time for me to walk away.

There was a good reason editors and agents became writers themselves but publicists rarely did. In the age of the pitch call, it was an impossible situation. What started out as a nice problem to have (*Local Girl Makes Good!*) became a real problem to have. Every interview kicked off with the question of whether my authors were irritated with me for publishing a book of my own, a mostly laughable idea at Knopf. But occasionally it was true enough. Inside the office, I was being watched for signs of negligence. Outside the office, I was a novelty act. At one point, a books columnist told me he had room to cover either the book I'd written or the book I was calling to promote. I should pick.

The morning I quit, Russell came into my office, asking if I thought we should send an author to the Midwest for her book tour. I put my head between my knees and started to cry.

"So that's a no to Minneapolis?"

He was horrified. We'd made it through a decade of bomb scares and budget cuts, of layoffs and literary controversies, and I'd never lost it. What was wrong? Was it my parents? A man? Had I finally *killed* a man?

I took a deep breath and raised my eyes to meet his.

"Oh, *God*," he said, slamming the door behind him.

As I hold the pieces of a ceramic drawer in place with one hand, waiting for the glue to dry, I answer e-mail with the other. I am curious to find out how well I can function in the hours immediately following the burglary, knowing in advance what the answer will be: fine. No one is the first person to whom bad things have happened. Functionality is not the problem. The problem is that our capacity to handle something shocking in the short term can make things indistinguishable in the long term. You become numb when you swallow too much sadness at once. The reason it feels like no boundaries have been crossed is because the concept of boundaries has been obliterated. Maybe there is no such thing as an emergency. Maybe our days are not a mixture of upbeat and downbeat songs, but notes in the same maudlin song. You just haven't hit the bridge yet. Keep humming, you'll get there.

People such as myself, who have mostly encountered anticipated trauma, "this is really going to hurt" trauma, are likely to find ourselves agape at the proximity of the ordinary to the extraordinary. The idea that misfortune arrives "out of the blue" means that the surrounding events become consequential in order to buttress the presence of the intruding event. You look back on the day of your car accident and remember how you broke a glass in the sink that morning. You never break glasses in the sink. What can be gleaned from this fact? To a person who does not expect trauma? Something cosmic. To a person who expects trauma? More or less nothing. Though, this state is not without its utility. As the poet Rainer Maria Rilke put it: "The person who has not at some point accepted with ultimate resolve and even rejoiced in the absolute horror of life will never take possession of the unspeakable powers vested in our existence."

For years, my most frequently cited example of this metamorphosis from wide-eyed to world-weary was when my uncle left my aunt. She came home on their twenty-fifth anniversary to find that, in addition to packing up all his belongings, he'd relieved the paper towel roll from its dispenser. If you asked my aunt to tell this story in the months that followed, the paper towel roll would be the constant detail, always delivered in the same flabbergasted tone. As if to say: What is this doing in the story? Get it out of the story. But years later, she knows: It is the story. It's all the same story.

The day Russell died, he posted a picture of wildflowers on Instagram. "Rudbeckia running rampant along the north side of the barn," he wrote. I suppose it's a sign of our times that his last written words are in the form of a caption. *Rudbeckia running rampant.* What a pleasant series of sounds. It's tempting to connect the photograph with what happened later that evening. That way the subsequent horror is not so out of the blue. That way the extraordinary has an on-ramp. It's tempting to reach through the screen, place a palm against the barn wall, and whisper: *Don't*. But it's just a picture he took before he left the house.

Thanks to my super, news of the burglary spreads fast. One agog neighbor asks if they took anything. No, they staged a sock puppet show and left. The eight-year-old downstairs is succinct in her sympathy. She tapes a note to my door that reads, "I feel bad for you." Another neighbor launches into the time someone stole his car radio. His story has the benefit of preparing me for what's to come, for people who seem offended when I am not interested in the vast prism of human experience. But I feel no kinship with those whose childhood homes were robbed. I feel even less with those who failed to take their laptops with them to the café bathroom. I feel something like disgust with those whose dorm rooms were looted, whose CDs vanished.

I try to think of a way I could care less about these people's stories and I succeed: I wish they'd been relieved of more possessions then, for having the gall to bring this up now. Make no mistake, the violation aspect of a burglary is real. It's no fun to lock your windows every time you take out the trash, to assume every creak in the floorboards has your name on it. Even before the cops arrived, I knew I'd be sleeping in my apartment that night—a psychological battle was coming and I refused to lose it, not in this economy. But also real is the fact that people hide behind violation because it eliminates the hierarchy of loss in their favor. They foist this belief on me, as if the jewelry is a minor concern. But the violation is the part of the space shuttle that breaks off so that the greater loss can go the distance.

I used to tease Russell about anthropomorphizing clocks and lamps, for treating the flea market like his personal orphanage. He believed in the souls of objects. It's where so much of his emotion lived, in these annexes of textiles and glassware, the miscellany of other people's lives. Items without a home made him restless. It was not enough for you to hold the porcelain ashtray shaped like a flamingo, you had to agree on its greatness. As someone who has refused to house extra copies of her own books, I never understood this.

For a while, I am only this. When a friend suggests I stay in her home, I don't get it. Who will stand guard if I'm gone? Who will conduct the hourly inventory? Then my pendulum swings in the *opposite* direction. Instead of herding objects, I get a little loose with them. In one week, I lose an umbrella, a pair of headphones, a laundry card, a phone charger, several lighters, a book, and a scarf. I forget a bag of groceries at the supermarket checkout. I mail letters without stamps. I leave my phone on someone else's nightstand. I also can't seem to hold on to my wallet. I donate it to a bar, then to my therapist's office. What my wallet was doing out at my therapist's office, I do not know. It's not a bodega.

Then one day, my phone rings in my pocket. It's the detective in the gray suit. It turns out there's security footage of the outside of my building. Cameras "caught something" the day of the burglary and he's coming over to review it. I sprint home and meet him in my super's apartment, a sanctum I have never before entered.

"Did you think of more?" asks the detective, while my super cues up the tape.

"More of what?"

"Any leads?"

"Isn't that my line?"

"This is terrible," my super pipes in.

He is bereft that this happened on his watch. He is the eyes and ears of this building. In the mailbox area, he once taped up two near-identical photos of the building and wrote "1987/2017!" in Sharpie, as if the change in awning color was of anthropological importance. For months, every time he sees me, he will go over what we saw on the security footage like he's Oliver Stone watching the Zapruder film. He physically reenacts the whole thing, sometimes getting so into it that he pretends to be the thief, pressing down on my shoulders and "scaling" me. I have to formally ask him to stop doing this.

The detective presses play: A man with a backpack paces outside the building, talking on the phone. He looks left. He looks right. When the coast is clear, he slips through the service gate. He saunters past the recycling bins and scampers up a not-insignificant brick wall. It's so graceful, I blurt out a nervous laugh. Once he's facing the back of the building, he has several options available to him, including the ground-floor apartments. He ignores them. Instead, he stares up at my apartment, leaps onto my fire escape and out of sight. A mere five minutes later, we watch him do the whole thing in reverse.

"Yikes," says my super, breaking the silence.

I can feel the pressure drop in the room. I ask him to go back to the part where the thief exits. Slow it down. Slower. *There.* What the heck is he doing?

The three of us squint. He is snapping off a latex glove. Not only will there be no fingerprints, but the footage has offered a far more disquieting piece of news: It is not lucky I wasn't home. Someone came for me, someone saw me leave, someone who knew where I lived. And I do not make a habit of embroidering my apartment number on my clothing. I was being watched. Or, as the detective puts it, "targeted." *Targeted.* The linguistic happy point between Observed and Stalked.

Here now, is where the Insanity, ready to party, enters the story.

Everyone's a suspect. Was it someone on drugs or after drugs? Was he hired? Had I undertipped a deliveryman who had a wildly disproportionate reaction? Every theory is problematic or absurd. None of this makes sense. Something is missing. Forty-one somethings, to be exact. And what if I had come home earlier? What then? There's such relief on other people's faces when I tell them I wasn't home. They assume a timeframe that exceeds forty-eight hours. Or twenty-four. Or one.

Russell tries to cheer me up by buying me glasses of alcohol. Like everyone else, he seems excited about the prospect of solving a mystery, by the burglary as a good story. Unlike everyone else, he seems resigned to the fact that it will never actually be solved. He offers to comb the flea market for me, but delivers the suggestion like a teenager working at an outlet mall: *I mean, we can give you ten percent off your next purchase. If you want.* He knows what's done is done. For most people, the story lives outside their conception of normalcy. The burglary arrived "out of the blue." But for all of Russell's surface joy, there is a well of darkness inside him, a pond that he can dip his hand into whenever he likes. It's not such a nice world. Bad things happen. Sometimes they happen all at once.

He listens attentively but calmly, nodding along. There will be no audible gasps from him. Good, I think. I don't need to be one more person's cocktail fodder. In return, I let him spew his cockamamie theory that the burglary is the master plan of my neighbors in the brownstone directly behind my apartment building. For years, their hard-partying teenager has been my *nemesis*.

"You think the people in the ten-million-dollar house hired someone to steal my prom jewelry? That sounds logical to you?"

"I'm surprised you don't think that," he says, unflinching.

"I don't know," I muse at the ceiling, "I kinda like the Seamless guy for this."

I play detective, partly because I have to and partly because I am living in a crime scene. I have two missions: find the jewelry and find the man who took it. I work freelance.

I mail photographs to a hundred pawnshops, visiting some in person. One pawnbroker tells me I have a solid "battle instinct," which inspires me to pound more pavement, to press more buzzers. Pawnbrokers are downbeat but agreeable. We chat, exchange pleasantries, I tell them to have a good time at their cousin's wedding. I set up alerts online. I have no way of gauging the expertise of the thief so I keep my parameters vague, plugging in "green" and "ring" and scrolling through thousands of photos until my phone reads: "Looks like you've reached the end."

Did you know you can reach the end of the Internet? Well, you can.

The thief had a plastic ID card clipped to his pocket, so I ask around at hospitals, hotels, and construction sites. No one can help me. And yet? No one can stop me. One day, on the way out of my building, I spot a man who is the physical opposite of the thief in every way, leaning on some scaffolding. Why so much leaning? I make it three blocks before giving in to the urge to run back. I bolt up the stairs and fling open my apartment door. The cat, she blinks.

The burglary is a tornado, ripping up insecurities, exposing their roots. This is all my fault for not moving homes or cities, for not taking certain jobs or marrying certain men, for looking backward all the time when I should be looking forward. I dwell too much. I hold on to things I shouldn't, to people I shouldn't. If you don't change, change will find you in its most unruly form. It will press down on your vulnerabilities until they squish out the edges. Life needs volunteers or else it will start calling on people at random. I promise to change. If only someone will take away the mental block that keeps me from solving this one mystery, from answering this one question, I promise to move forward. What is the behavior I have justified so well that I can no longer identify it as courting punishment? Is it the standard block that prevents any of us from knowing how the world sees us? *Pictures should be of what you see, not of what the world sees when it sees you.*

Perhaps, I think, the thief had a lookout.

I leave word at the coffee shop across the way, requesting that the manager take a look at his security footage. He calls me that afternoon and says that, actually, there *is* something suspicious. Two beefy-looking gentlemen came in thirty minutes before the burglary and sat by the window facing my building. One of them ordered a blueberry muffin. The other didn't order anything because . . . because . . .

He can't say the words. It's all too horrible.

". . . because he came in with a Starbucks cup."

I'm no legal expert but I'm fairly certain this makes this person guilty of going to Starbucks. Still, the manager insists on e-mailing me the video.

The suspects are wearing rugby shirts with horizontal stripes. Their arms are covered in tattoos. One of them has a reflective earring. They look like bouncers. I am in my bathrobe, sitting on the floor, six minutes into watching footage of two grown men sharing a muffin, when I decide I can't go on like this.

A grief support group seems at once dramatic and doable. I won't be so proprietary about the burglary around other burglarized people. It will feel good to show deference the second anyone says "masked" or "gunpoint." But when I look for a place to go, I can't find one. There are spaces, some literal and some virtual, for those left behind by cancer, heart attacks, natural disasters, and acts of terrorism. There are conversations meant for widows and parents and children. But there are no bereavement groups for *stuff*. They don't exist. I'm sorry your house blew up but it was only a house.

Grief is for people, not things. Everyone on the planet seems to share this understanding. Almost everyone. People like Russell, and people like me now, we don't know where sadness belongs. We tend to scrape up all the lonely, echoing, unknowable parts of ourselves and drop them in drawers or hang them from little wooden shelves, injecting our feelings into objects that won't judge or abandon us, holding on to the past in this tangible way. But everyone else? Everyone else has their priorities straight.

At long last, a measure of comfort comes from an unexpected place.

My friend Charlotte invites me to have dinner with her parents. I agree because they are not my parents and because the restaurant is close to the apartment that I apparently must guard at all times. They bring up the burglary with the caveat that I don't have to talk about it if I don't want to. Again: not my parents. I get halfway through the story before I notice that Charlotte's mother is rapt. A similar thing happened to her. I gird myself for more dorm-room drama.

When her children were small, she explains, they lived in a building that employed a window washer. One day, the window washer announced that he would be leaving the window-washing company and going out on his own and would Charlotte's mother still employ him? Of course, she said, she would. But a few weeks later, when she looked for the brooch her grandmother had brought over from Sweden when she immigrated, it had vanished. She could never prove this man was the culprit and he was now untraceable through his former employer. Still, she kept looking. Five years later, when she read how he was convicted of an unrelated crime, she drove to Rikers, where she sat in the waiting room for half a day.

"They refused to get a message to him," she says, "and I said, 'That's fine, I'll wait here.'"

Finally, a guard relented. He agreed to convey only one question: What happened to it? That's all she wanted to know. She was not going to press charges. He was already in prison. She just wanted to know.

Everyone else at the table has moved on, having heard this tale before. They are tearing at pizza and conferring with the waiter about wine. But I am on the edge of my seat. One of us is a septuagenarian Swedish woman, but we are both descended from immigrants. Maybe it's not that we loved these objects too much but that they are all the proof we have of the people who came before us.

"And then," she says, "the guard returned."

"And?"

"He said the window washer popped out the jewels and melted the rest. He took it apart, piece by piece."

Her voice cracks, her eyes fill with tears. This happened thirty years ago. A feeling of both horror and relief comes over me. It's surprising how harmoniously they snap together. As if by magic, I can see every last item in the thief's backpack. Anything plastic or resin is in the trash. The amber necklace is being fenced as we speak. Smaller pieces, like childhood charms, are being melted. But the green dome ring? Plucked apart with a pair of pliers. I'd been so desperate to go back to the evening of June 27, when I walked into my bedroom. What did you know? *Come on, what did you know?* At long last, I have found myself in a moment with the same frequency as that first moment. And I knew three things:

I knew I was the only apartment hit.

I knew I would never see that ring again.

I knew that I must learn to be okay with never knowing why.

Three nights before Russell dies, I take him out to dinner. He's agreed to stay with my geriatric cat while I'm at a literary festival in Australia, and he's come to my neighborhood to get a free lobster roll and a lesson in feline appetite stimulants. He pretends to be put out by this, but he's always had a thing for the cat. He is, after all, the only one who knows her e-mail password.

Even after all this time, it's odd to watch him take off his shoes and sit on my furniture, to know he'll be sleeping in my bed, chastising me for my sparsely stocked fridge. My old boss, his hair more salt than pepper now. We are sometimes taken aback by our relationship, which is both over- and ill-defined. We are not husband and wife. We tend to think the other is exaggerating when we gripe about our families, as neither of us has been forced to spend holidays with these people. I am not his person. He has a person. And yet? Every man I have ever dated has felt the presence of a second father, and his partner has felt the presence of a daughter.

During dinner, Russell orders what I order. At first, the talk is casual. His nephew will be visiting the city soon and Russell has promised to show him around. What do I suspect a twenty-year-old likes to do and eat? I shrug. Hookers and hot dogs? We move on to the topics of work and homelife. Neither are going very well but neither have been going very well for some time. Russell acknowledges he is not "easy" to live with, that this is a mild way to put it, but he has never had much interest in change. Inertia pervades and he is, as usual, dismissive of suggestions for resolution. We each have our lily pads of discontent. Mine center around romance and the end of the world. Russell's center around romance and the end of the publishing world. When I express a moony view of my years working on the other side of our industry, he insists that what I remember no longer exists. Modern life has closed in on it. Pieces of it have been falling from the ceiling for years. How have I not noticed? I drop it.

After dinner, he walks me home. As we part ways, he asks for an update on the burglary and I share my latest revelation. I will never find the dome ring because it no longer exists. It was his favorite. He liked to hold it up to the light and look at it from underneath. He said the setting resembled the ceiling of a miniature museum, maybe the Musée d'Orsay in Paris. He'd joke about me trading him the ring in exchange for gossip, in exchange for a promotion, in exchange for his egg roll. But the ring, I'd say, wasn't worth not having a grandmother. We don't *actually* think a thing can replace a person . . . do we? He'd smile and shoot back with: Jewelry is the answer to a riddle. What gets old but never ages?

It's getting late. The street is empty. The restaurant closed up around us. They were not subtle about it.

"If it's any consolation," he says, hugging me, "you can't take it with you when you go."

These are the last words he will ever say to me.

A few nights later, on Saturday, July 27, Russell is up in

Connecticut. He takes the dogs for an evening walk while his partner reads on the porch. He lets the dogs back into the house, through a screen door I can hear banging if I really want to. Then he turns on the television in the living room and leaves once more, moving across the yard. At eye level are his beloved chickens, asleep in their coop. They are named after a mix of former coworkers and dead celebrities ("Lana Turner almost pecked your eyes out this weekend"). Down the slope is the garden with the rhubarb no one eats. Buried in the ground are the rows of garlic he plants every year. Then he walks into the barn and hangs himself from a rafter.

It's hard to know the size of things. To manage the size of things. Am I making our friendship bigger than it was to keep it from getting any smaller? Making the robbery smaller than it was to keep it from getting any bigger? Am I projecting shared meaning onto completely unassociated events? It's not such a nice world. Bad things happen. Sometimes they happen all at once. Everything is muddled. I feel confused in the medical sense, like a side effect on a bottle. Intellectually, I know that if this must be the story, of a felony followed by a suicide, it should have separate entrances: one for the fly and one for the elephant. This is certainly how it will be in the future. Perspective will be painful but effortless. One day there will be only Russell and, on occasion, if I tell the story for long enough, a burglary that happened "around the same time." But we are so far from the future.

Right now, every time I try to separate these losses, to keep the first from contaminating the second, they come back together like magnets. Hideous sisters, they are keeping each other company in the dark. They are in conversation with each other. Sometimes I'm privy to the conversation, sometimes I'm not. They have their own language.

The author I admired, the one whose e-mail Russell forged, was Joan Didion. The day I learn he's dead, a detail from *The Year of Magical Thinking* comes rushing back to me. Shortly after Didion's husband dies, Julia Child dies. Didion expresses relief. She has a "sense that *this was finally working out*" because now Julia and John could have dinner together. At the time, I found it difficult to believe she actually thought that. "Had I been operating in my rational mind," she writes, "I would not have been entertaining fantasies that would not have been out of place at an Irish wake." But I now find myself in the throes of a similar fantasy. In this fantasy, Russell is the one who finds the jewelry. Because in this fantasy, there's a lost-and-found section of heaven where the dead can sift through missing objects and take what they want. This way they have something to love and those things are loved again. This way they get old but never age.

I think we would press the button at the same time, that's what I think.

It's Monday morning and I am leaving my therapist's office on the Upper East Side when I get the call. When I see "Russell (home)" pop up on my phone, I know it's not him. It's 9:38 a.m. Russell likes to get to the office early so that he can spend the rest of the day alternating between casually tormenting his staff and giving them candy. He's not in Connecticut, he can't be. Although perhaps I wouldn't know. It's been a long time since we were on the porch together, since I opened every drawer in the kitchen, hunting for a spoon. All my friends know of Russell; a good half have never met him.

I let the call go to voice mail. I know something is wrong. Just not how wrong. Do I go back upstairs? I should eat breakfast first. If Russell has been fired, I will need a layer of bread in my stomach before we start drinking. If he is in a coma, when he wakes, he will be amused to know that I swallowed a croissant whole, like a pelican. So this is what I do, buy a greasy pastry from a coffee cart. Russell had a theory that the best weight-loss plan was to simply avoid consuming any foods you wouldn't also rub on your face. I want to laugh, thinking of him saying this, but I can't. Something is wrong.

Before I can return the call, the phone rings again. This time, I pick up. It's Russell's partner, who asks if I'm alone.

"And what are *you* wearing?"

I can sense how inappropriate this joke will be in a matter of seconds. But if I say what I'd normally say, maybe nothing will be wrong.

I am told. Time does not stop but it rises, becoming out of reach. Mostly, I am trying to compute how such a big story fits into my ear. My first impulse is to try pretending this is an old truth, that Russell died a long time ago. Or that I never knew him. Or that neither of us was ever born. If I go back far enough, I can yank the story out at the root. I run to a trash can to vomit.

Afterward, I sit on the sidewalk like a senile dog. People are staring. At some point, I get up and walk west, through Central

Park, looking up at the trees. *Do you have anything to say for yourself, trees? No, of course not. You live to expand, not retract. Suicide is above your pay grade.*

On the other side of the park, I drift toward my old apartment building. I sit on the stoop, making calls, ruining the days of people who should not hear about this online but might not hear about it otherwise. Selfishly, I want witnesses, people to confirm this is happening. But I also know this is what Russell would do if the roles were reversed. He turned me into a good publicist, so much so that, even now, in this terrible moment, I can't shake the need to frame the story. To make it digestible for others even as I am still digesting it myself. I light a cigarette between calls, blowing the smoke up at my old window. Russell rented a studio apartment around here, farther uptown. He commuted to the office from that apartment during the week, instead of going back and forth to Connecticut. When it was warm out, he'd walk me home. When it was cold out too. I can see him so clearly, gliding over those hexagons of pavement framing the park, me pleading with him to slow down.

"Where do you need to be in such a hurry?"

"Nowhere, but I'd like to get there this century!"

There are his leather shoes, moving so fast his feet resemble the bottoms of rocking chairs. He wore the soles down until they talked. Now here are the shoes again, yanked into the air. I press my forehead against the railing of the stoop until it hurts. Behind me, the door opens and shuts several times. Pairs of shins move up and down the stairs, giving me a wide berth. Strangers. Strangers who can spot the difference between a bad day and a break in a life. I would like to tune out their thoughts but they hook into my skin, pulling as they pass. Maybe one of these people lives in my old apartment. Maybe I could go inside, crawl under a blanket, wake up in my old life. If the previous tenant of my current apartment buzzed up and explained that, for reasons he would not be disclosing, he needed to take a semi-annual nap on my sofa, I'd let him.

I'd say, "Of course, wind back the clock, say no more."

A submission to future editions of *The Book of Questions*:

> You and a person you love deeply are sitting in a room, looking at a door. It's been established that the door does not open from the inside. One day, the other person gets up and, without a word, waltzes out the door. What would you do?

I take the 6:01 a.m. train up to Connecticut to see Russell's partner. My phone is flooded with texts from mutual friends and former coworkers (often the same set of people), concerned about Russell's partner. There is the idea of an open portal. Of an alternative to this one. Of a man on the edge. There are whispers. Are we being dramatic? I don't know and refuse to find out. I will not be asking a man, the week his partner dies, what his big plans are for the summer. I catch sight of my reflection in the window. Look at that sad woman on a train, I think. I am wearing a pair of dark sunglasses that Russell liked.

"Like a Jewish Jackie O.," he decided.

"Wasn't Jackie a little Jewish?"

"Just take the compliment."

I can't take the compliment. The minutes keep coming and I cannot swat them away. I sit in this earthly lump I cart around, hating my eyes fixed in their sockets, hating my heart, so showy in its persistence. I wish I could ball up my skin, drop it under the seat, and watch it roll away. I, too, am the subject of whispers.

His partner and I never make it out of the parking lot. We don't go to the house or to a restaurant. Security footage would show me opening the car door and, a couple of hours later, getting out.

What can be done with this part of the story? With the details shared? This is the room I don't show people, pulling the door closed as I pass. *Oh, this? Laundry room. Broom closet.* All the love I have for Russell cannot erase what he allowed his partner to see, what he wanted his partner to see. The brutality. The vindictiveness. The time it must have taken to get him down. The time between the discovery and the call, between the call and the coroner. Russell has split himself into two people: Dead Russell and Alive Russell. It's too many Russells. One was a handful. His partner and I sit, sobbing side by side. We muse about the mail. Russell liked to sign up for catalogs using the dogs' names. Thirty percent off cookware for dogs. Two-for-one lingerie discounts for dogs. Like the minutes, those will keep coming.

When you die by suicide, you die alone. With few exceptions, you die alone. I don't think people talk about this enough when they talk about suicide, if they talk about it at all. The ending of one's life is the thing. Taking attendance seems like splitting hairs. But I cannot get over it. My friend was alone when he was murdered. I repeat it out loud, opting for a purposefully skewed angle on the story and scanning for errors. The facts check out. My friend was alone when he was murdered. I don't quite have the ego to think I could've stopped a cogent fifty-two-year-old man with no history of depression or therapy and no prior attempts at self-harm from taking his own life. Still, there are those who will, unsolicited, tell me that I shouldn't blame myself. These people are idiots. Or else they are projecting their own losses.

And are also idiots.

I am angry. It's too soon to be this angry. I know the stages of grief are not linear, nor are they solid enough to be hidden under shells and slid around, but something is off. Russell and I did not share young children, a mortgage, or a business. But then I realize: This anger is a false positive. I am not angry at *Russell*. I am angry at everyone *except* for Russell.

A guy on a Citi Bike rounds a corner and stops so close, he hits my wrist. When he won't apologize, I run after him, suggesting he go fuck his mother. My super, who tends to make conversation by scolding people, knocks on my door to lecture me about a package I've left languishing on the lobby radiator for an hour. Instead of thanking him and moving on, I snap at him. This panic about everyone's belongings is a little late, don't you think? Don't take the burglary out on *me*, I tell him (even though I am, at present, taking Russell's death out on him). Later, I will feel shame about this interaction.

I start shutting out friends. With some, I can't stand to see my pain reflected in their eyes. There are craters in their timelines, as well, ancient holes in the shape of someone gone too soon. But I don't want to be around more entrenched versions of myself. I barely want to be around this version. Others knew Russell the same way I did, worked with him too, spent those summers on his porch too. But we have all committed the sin of not being able to bring him back. Still others offer me pat wisdom that sounds as if it's been vetted by general counsel. I can tell I'm being *handled*. They assure me I won't feel like this forever. Oh, yeah? Everyone's a psychic when you're sad. With more casual connections, I've always held the watering can of our two-person garden and now I can put it down. If all it takes is one unanswered text to kill the friendship, then that's all it takes. When a newer friend hears the news secondhand, she calls, but there's a strange racket in the background. She's bottling vinegar. Lots of vinegar. Unholy amounts of vinegar. I comment on the cacophony of glass, hoping she will take the hint. Is this the best soundtrack for the annals of a hanging? But the noise shows no sign of abating. She's multitasking a condolence call.

"I can't do this," I say, and hang up on her.

For everyone's safety, I decide it's easier to seek out people who aren't aware of the burglary or the suicide, people I know from "around" who will surely gloss over these major bummers. Because New York is home to the largest population of narcissists outside Los Angeles, most of us have a contingency of acquaintances who are entertaining but impervious to empathy. These are the people I choose to stay out with until 4:00 a.m. The quicker they reveal how their father's law partner's wife killed herself in 1980, the better I feel. More, more, more. I have perfectly edible yogurt in my fridge, purchased before my best friend hanged himself, but do go on. Their stories distract me. This time, I *am* interested in the vast prism of human experience, but only because I am a vampire, sucking on the necks of other vampires. Only one question stops me: Did you know?

I know this is shorthand for a need to manage chaos, to usher in a sense of coherence, but we should consider eliminating it as a reaction to suicide. "Did you know?" is not about the person who died. It's about asking for permission to add Russell to the files of stories we all keep about jettisoned medications and erratic behavior. Because if I have a crystal ball, maybe we all have crystal balls. Maybe others can use me to inoculate themselves. Maybe I can teach them to make the signs appear. *See how clipped his recent e-mails were? There you have it.* Ideations notwithstanding, I find it hard to believe any suicidal person knows the exact dimensions of what they're hiding. So why would the rest of us have a superior sense? And who among us is categorically happy? Rather, who among us is categorically happy and tolerable? Who lacks a reason to kill themselves? Reasons are not the problem.

Part of the destigmatization of suicide is not framing the desire, or even the flirtation, as exceptional. If the major religions are less horrible about it than they used to be (not as much dragging of bodies through streets these days), we should do better too. Suicide is a tax on human consciousness. Most people pay this tax in undetectable denominations. Like wondering what would happen if they stand too close to the cliff's edge or thinking "don't jump" as the train comes charging down the tracks—they fear the mere option will override their free will. But some pay this tax dearly. Some pay it with their lives. The question everyone should therefore ask is not why otherwise healthy people kill themselves but why they themselves should go on living.

That sentence will surely read as morbid to those who have never identified as depressed and disconcerting to those who know me personally. But it's no threat to anyone's psychological soundness to think this way. We all have something we're trying to fend off. The question is how big and with what?

There's a scene in the movie *The Big Chill* in which the dead character's friends are trying to make sense of his suicide. They ask his girlfriend if he was acting strangely before he slit his wrists. "I haven't met that many happy people in my life," she responds. "How do they act?" I think of this line when I think of Russell, just as I think of the figurine he kept on his desk, of a man with swirls for eyes. The base read: "You don't have to be crazy to work here but it sure helps!" The miracle of life is not that we have it, it's that most of us wake up every day and agree to fight for it, to hold it in our arms even when it squirms to get away. It's a miracle, a genuine miracle, that the reverse doesn't happen more often. Or, to quote Russell's favorite film, *The Lion in Winter*: "Of course he has a knife, he always has a knife, we all have knives."

During a short-lived but potent superstitious phase, it takes me forever to leave the house. This is because of all the crap I have to kiss or touch or bring with me so that more bad things don't happen. So that nothing else goes missing. I lock my windows. I check the doorknob. I open and close the drawers of the spice cabinet. Still empty. I was wearing the same bright orange dress the day of the burglary as I was the night Russell and I had dinner. When he walked into my apartment, he pushed past me and said: "Why are you dressed like a traffic cone?"

I decide the dress is damned and shove it down the garbage chute.

Along with the superstition comes the paranoia. Russell did not battle with a demonstrable disease, going in and out of treatment, just like I did not lose my rings one by one. Anyone can have her batteries taken out midmarch. I once interviewed Mariel Hemingway about a documentary she'd made about her family's history with mental illness. She counted seven suicides off the top of her head, including her grandfather. She said that when her sister died, she was scared she would be next, not because she was suicidal but because she felt suicide was sentient, not just familial. It needed a host body. I didn't compute this at the time. But now the idea of suicide as contagious, as a baton pass, comes naturally.

Now that Russell is dead, I can label this state of perpetual vigilance as I could not before. Rather, a professional can. What I am experiencing is post-traumatic stress disorder. PTSD employs a math opposite to that of denial: Instead of your brain convincing itself nothing has happened, it convinces itself everything has and is still happening. Which could explain why I start doing head counts, calling up everyone I've ever known who's been depressed, to see if they're okay. Half my friends are writers, the other half work with writers. This takes days.

One of my calls is to a friend who suffers from severe clinical depression. He's participated in clinical trials, checked himself into specialized hospitals, dabbled in transcranial magnetic stimulation. But he assures me I shouldn't worry.

GRIEF IS FOR PEOPLE | 49

"I've always wanted my life to be different," he says, "not over."

"Okay," I say, "good."

Alas, my relief upon hearing this is fleeting. There's a Korean saying that goes like so: You have nothing to fear from someone who threatens he is going to kill you tomorrow. I wonder how, if at all, this idea applies to suicide. I have friends who've been known to send histrionic texts about how the cards are stacked against them, about how "done" they are with everything. Friends who scan every assurance for holes where the dark can crawl back in. This is how they process the severity of their feelings, by inducing panic in others. But just because you think the world revolves around you doesn't mean you're thrilled about it. According to the Korean saying, and according to my clinically depressed friend, such people are safe from suicide because . . . because why? Because they would've done it by now? That makes no sense. Is it therefore the people who have never expressed a suicidal thought that warrant our concern? That's most of the population.

I wanted so badly to be like Russell, and maybe now I can be. He banked his pain in some secret place where no one could see it, and maybe I can do the same. Maybe I can put mine in a cabinet. But the drawers keep popping open. The grief does not cotton to being squished. It takes the form of painful blooms in the chest that require attention, often in public. I stop in the street, putting my hand over my heart like I've just remembered something. Or else I sit on planes with tears streaming down my face.

"The oxygen levels," I explain to the stranger across the aisle, who agrees but thinks better of it: "But the plane hasn't taken off yet."

There's a translucent membrane around everything, a bubble that moves with every step. Russell is so close, right on the other side. Like the ring trapped inside my pinkie, I have the strongest sensation that if I only knew where to push, I could reach through and pull him back. The bubble hardens with each passing day. By living, I am, by default, leaving him.

I am disgusted by the universal truths of grief, by the platitudes. I don't want to make my way through the coming stages, however ill-defined. I don't want to become more human for this experience. Whatever level of human I'm at is fine. I don't want to throw my psychic lot in with anyone else's, nor should those who've lost spouses and children have to throw their lot in with mine. Empathy comes from the same place but loss does not. This, I now understand, is why grief groups exist for people. They are populated by those who do *not* want to be there, not by those who do. No one sitting in a folding chair needs to be convinced of her suffering. No one comes to be cowed by the worseness of someone else's story. This is especially true of suicide, a death so common it's a public health crisis. And yet, no two are alike. A march for whatever killed Russell, and Russell alone, wouldn't last a city block.

The one thought that comforts me during this time is a controversial one: I don't believe Russell thought he'd lost his argument with life; I believe he thought he'd won it. He no longer saw a place for himself in the world and this was the same as a terminal illness. The illness of aging. The illness of aging as a gay man.

The threat of irrelevance, the loss of power, the expansion of indignities, the condition of being alive. All to be nipped in the bud before the symptoms got too gnarly, all to be addressed while he still had a choice. He had balanced his life and, in the words of Yeats, "The years to come seemed waste of breath, / A waste of breath the years behind." And who are we to litigate the severity of someone else's pain? Suicide is often referred to as a permanent solution to a temporary problem.

No one here is arguing the first half of that.

We like to speak of what the dead would've liked. We build totems and write poems when what most people would've liked is not to be dead. A person who dies by suicide does not fit so neatly into this paradigm. I keep reading poetry and philosophy, looking for answers, looking for wisdom beyond my limitations. But I know one thing the poets and philosophers don't: Russell.

If he were writing this instead of me, he would tell you that his suicide only feels tragic but is not, in itself, a tragedy. We all die. Agreed? He might then say that, taken as a matter of inevitability, the *burglary* is "worse" than the suicide because the burglary is neither universal nor voluntary. Russell and the German philosopher Arthur Schopenhauer (whose take on suicide went something like "my body, my choice") are probably dining together in heaven right now, Plato in the kitchen. Russell set himself free from unfathomable anguish. Even if you take the opposite view of things, of suicide as an eternal prison, well, it's just the one prisoner. There are plenty of other lost souls. Go save one of them. And, no offense, but it kind of doesn't matter *what* you think. Everyone will be sad about this for a month. Then life will return to normal. You'll see.

How difficult it is to love someone who was so wrong and who will never be right again.

The reason the kangaroo and the emu appear on Australia's coat of arms is because neither animal is capable of walking backward. The implication being that one must always look ahead, must progress into the future. For all of Australia's resolute lightness (here you will find the cheer of Southern California crossed with the repression of England), it has the substantial task of being the planet's emissary into the next day. Which, in theory, means Russell should be *more* dead here. But the second I set foot in Melbourne, I have the sensation of time running backward, of traveling back to when Russell was alive. And in this alternate world, I decide to tell not a soul of what has happened. I am playing a game called My Friend's Not Dead. It has one player.

What starts as a great effort not to spill my miserable wares soon turns me euphoric. Normally one to scurry back to my hotel room at any multipronged event, I will talk at length with anyone, about any subject. I say yes to every coffee, to letting my brain be picked over like a wombat carcass. I invite *most* people I meet to dinner in New York. I drive to a sculpture park with several authors, where we zigzag between manicured lawns, commiserating about jet lag. I read the names of the artists, using whatever part of my mind is responsible for letting information drift in before letting it drift right back out. I laugh easily and loudly, swinging between functionality and personality. Back in town, I jog through Victoria Gardens, grinning at cockatoos.

These guys know how to keep a secret. Good birds.

I nearly spoil things for myself by mentioning Russell to the cat sitter I now must hire. When she asks what happened, I offer a terse summary of events: *The old cat sitter killed himself.* She and I have a rapport, but not that strong a rapport. I follow up with: *I mean . . . just say you don't want to do it, right?* An ellipsis appears and then vanishes. There's no way for her to respond to that. Alas, I am not on her side. I am not on the side of the living, or the group Iris Murdoch called "the unbereaved." Here, in the small hours of grief, I am not to be trusted. I am no one's friend. I choose Russell above all others.

Reality starts to creep in during the convening of a book club. Six months prior, the festival had asked me to make an "American" selection for their book club. I chose Joan Didion's *Slouching Towards Bethlehem*. But when we sit in a circle, all anyone really wants to talk about are her pair of death memoirs, the books about her husband and her daughter. The consensus seems to be that these are far more personable than the essays, that Didion's tone is less detached. Perhaps there is no need for me to disagree, to say, actually, her tone is the same as always, if anything the style is stripped to the bone, it's the subject that's a mess. One woman suggests the memoirs were written so Didion could forgive her husband for "abandoning" her. Granted, this is not the first word I'd use, but the man sitting across from her has an outsize reaction. He speaks in a voice antithetical to the circle formation.

"What's to forgive?!" he shouts. "It's not like he killed himself."

Under normal circumstances, I'd want nothing to do with this person, but now I'd like to drag my chair over to this oracle in denim. Do you have to forgive a person who dies by suicide?

What if part of you is relieved for them? To be gobsmacked by suicide, to consider it in need of forgiveness, is a marker of solipsism, is it not? It's to deny what the world is like for others, to decide that darkness exists in service to light, that darkness is the glitch and lightness is the control. Because that's how it is for you. I want so badly to be like the kangaroo or the emu, to move forward through time, but I am angrier at the *jewelry* for allowing itself to be removed than I am at Russell. Do I have it all mixed up? Back in my hemisphere, no one will tell me if I have it mixed up because they feel sorry for me. Or because they think I'm crazy. Or because they're bottling vinegar.

During the closing lecture of the festival, a Scottish author winds down her reading with a folk song about the sea. Her voice is not like an author's. It's like a Merchant Ivory film that can sing. She lilts all over the stage. I imagine this moment holding me up on its hip, bouncing me. Wave goodbye to Russell! Say: Bye-bye, Russell! I can feel my heart pounding in my neck. Salt water drips down my face and I scratch my pinkie so hard, I nearly break the skin.

Darling, I think, *whatever have you done to yourself?*

On the plane home, I buy two rings, one silver and one gold. Russell had advised me to "get something classy for once." I'd planned on some kind of ritualistic first purchase. But with the length of the Pacific Ocean before me, I plug in a price range, click a few boxes, take a pill. I then have three dreams, none realistic yet all real to the point of lucidity. It's a dirty trick to cede a story to a dream, not to mention flirting with tedium. But it's now years into the future and these dreams remain so close to the surface of my memory, they don't feel like dreams at all. They feel like a set of parallel realities.

First comes the pale dream: I am walking along train tracks outside an abandoned city. The buildings in the distance have been hollowed out by bombs and the tracks are covered in sand, pushed into dunes by the wind. There's a tunnel in the distance and before it, a small wooden sign. When I come to the sign, I see it's blank. And yet, I can read it. It says that so long as I'm alive, this is as far as I will go.

Next comes the bright dream: In this dream, I am Russell. I check into a hotel in Hawaii. A concierge gives me a tour of my suite and points over the balcony, at the ocean, where I can see a few friendly fins breaking through the surface. She explains that in this place, sea creatures will appear in proportion to the happiness you need. When I look down again, Russell has split from me. I am on the balcony and he is splashing around in the water. He slides his goggles to his forehead and rubs his eyes. Manatees and dolphins appear around him. A flirtatious sea lion butts its head against his. I have concerns. Will he have to tread water like that for eternity? What if he drowns?

"He can't drown," says the woman, matter-of-factly.

The third and final dream is the only one I've ever had in black and white. All my jewelry has been put back except it looks like it's been gnawed on. The beads are cracked, the pearls are deflated as if by a needle. But it's recognizable enough and it's all over my apartment, dangling from lampshades, curled in glass jars, hanging on doorknobs. Even the dome ring is here, lolling around in a ceramic drawer.

I wake up in New York, eager to tell Russell the good news.

But both my items and my audience have vanished.

A week later, the new rings arrive. Two plain circles, I roll them across my desk. Poor rings, they live in the shadow of a mystery. Worse, they are guilty by association. What if, by some act of God, the old rings come back and I have to explain that these new rings mean nothing to me? But it's not so bad, having them here. It's satisfying to push them apart and slide them back together as I spend my days banging on the walls of this story, trying to find a way in so that I might find a way out. They remind me of the Girl Scouts song:

> *Make new friends but keep the old*
> *One is silver and the other gold*

I suppose the idea is that, given enough time, the silver friends will turn gold too. I don't know about that. But it's a trick I'd like to see.

PART II

OBJECT PERMANENCE

(BARGAINING)

Object permanence is the understanding that something exists, even if it's hidden. It's one of the earliest instances in which we use a child's partially formed brain to amuse them. Presumably, you would not knock a toddler off-balance for laughs, but peekaboo is the first game we play. How this experience is not horrifying for its victims, I have no idea. Something to which you've grown quite attached, be it a stuffed bunny or your mother's face, is now gone, potentially forever. Yet children are delighted by the concept. Maybe it's the suspense. Though who knows at what age one develops a narrative arc? Probably twenty-six. More likely, it's because if things didn't keep disappearing, they couldn't keep coming back.

The coming back is the best part.

In a bonus dose of misfortune, I happen to live on the same block as the restaurant where Russell and I shared our last meal. We dined in the corner where the windows meet. Which means that when I pass the place, which is unavoidable unless I never turn right, I can relive that evening. As if Russell's absence is easily explained by a trip to the restroom. Here are the high-backed chairs. Here is the waitress running a damp towel weirdly close to the torsos of patrons as they sit. Russell will appear at any minute, and when he does, he will not want to see me trespassing on the stoop across the street, where I sit, night after night, and talk to him in my head:

You do realize we're all going to get old and die without you? One day, I'll be fifty-two and you'll still be fifty-two. Which is some bullshit. Camus wrote that there is but one truly serious philosophical problem, and that is suicide. Having children doesn't qualify. It's the eradication, the going against the grain. And you know what George Sand said? George Sand said we cannot tear a single page from our lives but we can burn the whole book. Were you a George Sand person? I should be able to remember, since you loved or hated everything. Nothing was ever just okay. See? I'm forgetting you already. Here's one I know you like, from By Grand Central Station, I Sat Down and Wept: *"Why do I not jump off this cliff where I lie sickened by the moon? I know these days are offering me only murder for my future." The narrator becomes envious of a hawk because it can get away from Earth and she can't. You introduced me to that book. Now it's another piece of a puzzle you don't want me touching. No need to be so secretive. All the pieces are black. I'll never put it together.*

Every few minutes, someone will walk by, a dog leading the

way, and I will think: *The dogs. Everyone comes to it eventually. How could you have left the dogs? A common dumbfoundment in situations like these. But I find it too painful to believe you "left" the dogs. Because if you left the dogs, that means you left every lesser being too.*

In the most recent dream, Russell and I are sitting at a seaside café in the middle of winter, the scalloped edge of a table umbrella flipping up in the wind.

"What happened?" I ask him. "Just tell me what happened."

He bows his head and digs his fists into his pockets. A mutual friend walks up from the beach and starts to answer for him, but Russell covers his ears and screams at the top of his lungs: "No! No! No! No! No! I shouldn't be here for this!"

I savor the dreams as much as I dread them.

They are the only way I get to hear him say new things.

I would very much like to stop sitting on this stoop. But we have a problem: I don't know where he is. Russell doesn't have a gravestone. No forwarding address. And I can't bring myself to inquire about his ashes, it feels too crass, too much of a reminder of his dead body. As if his partner needs reminding. I am saddened by a restaurant but I don't have to wake up and go to sleep in a restaurant. My only job is to gather up all the pleasant images I can. Alas, his partner is not the logistical hub of this death. We have not spoken since that awful morning in Connecticut and not much more in the years before that. He was never as social as Russell (an insurmountable bar), but he'd begun retreating to his own private spaces, into his own rhythm, long before Russell died.

Perhaps the ashes are with his mother. Or his sister. Perhaps they are up at the house. Perhaps they were fed to the chickens. He really loved those chickens. Sometimes people will track me down and inquire about the whereabouts of the ashes. I tell them I don't know. I, too, have nowhere to go. I do not share my chicken theory with them.

The first time Russell and I came to this particular restaurant was after we'd seen a screening of *The Devil Wears Prada*. He predicted the movie would be a hit—it humanizes a difficult boss, it's a propaganda film for him—but a single flaw prevented him from loving it: It ended too many times.

"Hollywood movies used to just end and you didn't have to know everything," he explained. "It should've stopped when she quit her job and threw her phone into the fountain. But *oh no*, she has to make amends with the boyfriend and the coworker and get a new job and make meaningful eye contact with Meryl Streep . . ."

He was right. The movie takes too many bows. He was right an irritating amount of the time. Well, with one exception. Sometimes there aren't any bows. Sometimes you get to watch a stranger eat calamari in your dead friend's chair.

It's September 27, 2019. Seasonal betrayal is in the air. People have lives and the world needs to spin on, in order to accommodate them. If not them, their rituals, their weddings and their concerts and their conferences. I flirt with the idea of joining their ranks. You can let some things float away without putting your whole arm in the water. Russell was a French Exit person. He would vanish from parties, particularly if you'd agreed to leave with him but were taking too long to say your goodbyes. It was a form of punishment for allowing yourself to be detained by a new interaction. Turn around and he'd be gone. I am a Jewish Exit person (whereby one tracks down people with whom one hasn't spoken, expressly to inform them of one's departure). Maybe it's time to take a note from my friend.

Because something must be done. My initial grief, which I thought might be taking a manageable shape, has mutated. It's colonized my entire personality. Any word that comes out of my mouth that is not Russell's name is a lie. The missing is so constant, even I am surprised by it. And I am at ground zero of the missing. I eat too much or too little, vacillating between punishment and erasure. I drift off during conversations, engaging in fantasies in which I go up to Connecticut. As the train pulls in, I spot Russell on the platform, sleeping in the little shelter. I hold out my hand. *It was a mistake. People make mistakes. Let's get you home.* Therapy seems futile, as does travel, nature, sleep, television, music, comedy, theater, art, cooking, exercise, reading, and sex. For days on end, my heart beats rapidly and at inexplicable times. Five, six, twelve times a day this happens. A flat surface is preferable. Eventually, I see a cardiologist, who asks me questions as my body rats me out to her stethoscope.

Have I been smoking? Yes.

Drinking? Yes.

Caffeine? I write for a living.

Drugs? Nothing to write home about but I guess that depends on your home.

She arches her eyebrow. Anything else? Nothing comes to mind.

"It sounds like panic attacks. Have you experienced any unusual stress?"

I shake my head. The mourning has become such a constant, Russell's suicide no longer registers as out of the ordinary. I have eliminated the contrast between light and dark, dismantled the whole frame of reference.

"There is one thing."

"What's that?"

"A home invasion," I offer, "but back in June and I wasn't there."

Only as I button my shirt do I mention the suicide, as if she already knows.

"How will he know you loved him," she asks, "unless you try to destroy yourself?"

Back at my desk, I add this line to a document so brief, its contents double as the title of the document: "The Concept of Feeling Better."

Did I mean to suggest that sanity is a phenomenon? Or, simply, "is a good one"?

Loved ones suggest I take up a hobby. Silly gooses, I *have* a hobby. My hobby is drilling down to the core of Russell's suicide. But the drill bits keep snapping off. One night, drunk, I google "Russell," expecting only photos of him to appear. Another night, high, I google "how to conduct a séance," only to be met with articles on "how to throw a séance." I don't need a party that smells like sage. I need my friend back. I spend hours this way, dreaming up new ways to think of him, smacking at macabre piñatas. When his birthday rolls around, texts are bandied about among our friends. But every day is Russell's Dead Day in this house. And for what? Like the burglary, I sense that the most clear-eyed take I will have about this was in the moments directly following it. That understanding was a gift of proximity.

What I am experiencing is called cumulative grief, or "grief overload," the kind associated with multiple losses, often of different genres, always in quick succession. I do remember what it was like to concern myself with other matters. Sanity is on the horizon if only I am willing to put in the work. Not to force it, mind you—nothing seems to horrify people so much as the idea that you might rush the grieving process even as their tolerance for the topic dwindles—but maybe I can start by not peering into this restaurant every night like a goddamn chimney sweep.

"Enough," I say out loud, standing.

But then something happens. Something out of the blue. An e-mail from an address I don't recognize alerts me to its presence with a ding. I look down at my phone, which is already glued to my palm. This is because I am, in a very real way, waiting for Russell to call. The subject line reads: YOUR JEWELRY.

What would it be like to see your most cherished possessions for sale, possessions that you yourself did not put up for sale? The ghosts know, loitering over yard sales as they do. Naturally, I have seen photos of my jewelry prior to this moment. Mostly because I was in them. At the detective's request, I sent a few shots over the night of the burglary (I did this after I had my fingerprints taken, an unfortunate order of events for my keyboard). I also selected one to disseminate online. Asking social media for help is like playing Russian roulette except there's a bullet in most of the chambers. I was conscious of what might be perceived as a privileged or superficial loss, but happy enough to use my anatomy to stress the gravity of the situation. A man came into my bedroom. He was on my bed. Let us now wonder what *could* have happened. Probably nothing. Having the skill set for one violation doesn't give you the skill set for all of them. Or the desire. I don't buy butter if I pass a supermarket on the way to the airport.

The e-mail is from a gentleman who has attended some of my book readings. He is a welcome presence, a good egg. The Egg saw my tweet and felt sorry for me. Good, I think. I want people to feel sorry for me about the jewelry as much as I do not want them feeling sorry for me about Russell. The jewelry is in danger of being dismissed entirely, falling as it does in a category that includes smashed car windshields. Whereas with the suicide, I worry that I am becoming the recipient of a dead man's outreach. My newfound proximity to death means that confessions of past ideations and attempts are being shared with me because they can no longer be shared with Russell.

The Egg plugged his own criteria into eBay, a startling level of investment in someone else's woes. He knew it would be a tricky needle to thread but here we are, months later, and the thread has come out the other side. He copies the link to the seller's page and wishes me luck. *Signed, Egg.*

There are two listings.

One is for the amber amulet.

The other is for the tiger's-eye ring.

If Russell had taught me to anthropomorphize objects, I had, in turn, begun to think of this jewelry as dead. But the ring gives itself away. Years ago, the stone came loose and I had it repaired. The stripes went in vertical but came back horizontal, which happens to be very noticeable in tiger's eye. This means that not only are there a mere handful of this ring in existence, there is only one with the stripes running in the wrong direction. As if this weren't confirmation enough, there's the matter of the company it's keeping: an orange amulet that looks as if it once belonged to a wicked queen.

These are proof-of-life photos. In the amber, I can see the bright reflection of an overhead light fixture. Where are you, you unblinking pupil? According to the listing, somewhere in Brooklyn. The necklace is being sold for a whopping $4,950 by a seller with 98.4 percent positive feedback. The condition is "pre-owned" (I'll say!) and it does not come with a pouch (did too). The ring, on the other hand, has been appointed a pouch by the court. It sits on a scrap of blue suede with the Tiffany logo emblazoned on it. Clever. Unlike the necklace, the ring is not for sale. It's at auction. There are sixteen bidders.

There is an idea swirling around my skull, getting faster with each rotation and I am powerless to stop it. Every piece of jewelry—as well as every patch, matchbook, and pearl—is now contained within these two tiny artifacts. The green dome ring? There in spirit. The past six months? Also contained therein. My whole life in New York? Present. The suction is so strong, it takes something else from the past with it. Something bigger. It is not time to let Russell go, no sir. I feel like a traitor, thinking of that moment, not two minutes ago, when I entertained such ideas. I don't need sleep. I don't need a hug. All I need is to follow this trail. Because if I can get these items back, I can get my friend back.

I would sooner be separated from this logic than from my own skin.

My own skin. The ring probably still has my DNA on it. I feel like boxing it in the ears and dragging it home. That night, I watch the auction clock tick down into the wee hours. The ring costs me $68. Relinquishing money to people who stole from me (or, at minimum, feeding money into a system that allowed me to be stolen from) does not sit well. But I have not paid $68 for a ring.

I have paid $68 for a return address.

Can we ever get back what's lost? This is the question posed by a woman in my suicide survivor grief group, or, as another member dubs it, a "virtual grief group." Is the grief virtual or the group? Either way, during a particularly dark night, when a tsunami of wallowing has wiped out the possibility of a suitable person or professional to address it, I seek out the group. I log on for several nights in a row and then never log on again.

You can't linger in places like this. People attack you with love. You crowd-surf on the loving hands of strangers. Anytime you like, you can enter this collective mood; no need to read the room when the room reads you. But therein lies the danger. People become addicted to the foul weather of the group. One man addresses every comment within minutes. It's so consistent, I wonder if he's a bot. A grief bot? When a recently widowed woman confesses to having a breakdown after throwing out the plastic sandwich bags her husband used for his lunch (what if he's *in* the bags?), she gets a tome on the perils of domestic symbolism. I click on this man's profile. His bio explains how his teenage twins, a boy and a girl, died by double suicide a decade ago.

It's his hell, we're just living in it.

Most people in the group reply with a no. No, we can't ever get back what we've lost. You can cheat death sooner than you can cheat time. But some members of the group type "yes" and not for dramatic effect. Part of the frustration of suicide is that it undermines our sense of fairness. If someone can snatch themselves out of the world, it seems only right that we should be able to snatch them back into it. There's a reason the guidebook on suicide feels broad or written on the fly, attacked more from an ethical, social, or philosophical standpoint than a practical one. Because it is not shaped like "normal" loss, the idea of reversibility is at once preposterous and inherent in the act: If suicide is humanity's loophole, maybe the loophole can go both ways.

One of Russell's favorite books was Jean Stein and George Plimpton's oral biography of Edie Sedgwick, *Edie*, which is chockablock with privileged white people asphyxiating in cars and going at each other with steak knives. Everyone is such a pretty pancake, pounded into shape by good genes and inherited wealth, it can be hard to empathize with the weight of their legacy. It's as if they woke up one day and, instead of making cucumber sandwiches, decided to flick themselves or someone else off the planet. Edie herself overdosed on barbiturates. I don't suspect Russell glamorized *Edie*, the person or the book. There's no sign of imitation. He didn't do drugs. He hated pop art. But I believe his affection for the story is obliquely connected to his death.

Having grown up gay in a lower-middle-class enclave of New England, a former mill town where the rich know that ocean-front is oceanfront so long as you keep your back to the land, he longed for a more exclusive world. A more discriminating strain of the northeast. This is someone whose childhood hobby was writing letters to Hollywood actresses, asking for their auto-graphs, someone who walked out of *Manchester by the Sea* be-cause "I don't need a two-hour tour of my childhood." He was not taken with rich people, quite the opposite—he had a horror of the wealthy. His fascination was more to do with those who had the luxury of being eccentric. He was enchanted by magne-tism, which is not merely the ability to draw people in, but the substance to keep them there. He admired the definite way these well-funded personalities did things, including fall off the grid or dispatch themselves. Their whole lives, they could have any-thing they wanted. And now what they wanted was not to have lives.

The day before he died, a colleague gave him a framed poster of the original cover art for *Edie*. She found it while cleaning out her office. Russell hung it right away, going through the trouble of borrowing a drill from the maintenance department. Then he went home and never saw it again. If this is how Russell died, with forethought but also with a flick of the wrist (or what is known as "the impulsive act"), couldn't it just as easily not have happened? Really, why couldn't it not have happened? Why *can't* we get back what's lost?

I scroll through the answers: No. Yes. No. Yes. No. No.

Maybe. They look like responses to a customer service survey. *How likely are you to recommend this mourning experience?* Then the Bot King appears, putting a stop to the staccato replies: *You have to think about what you're asking. If you mean you have lost your life as you knew it and want it back, yes. That's what we all hope to do. Not to forget but to learn to live without. It's easy to slip into suffering alone. You don't have to do that. But can your loved one be returned to you in another form? I'd say that's almost impossible.*

Almost. *Almost* impossible.

My delusion is not exactly aided by the "survivor" label, which itches like a rental costume. Surely, these people can't mean *me*. I did not experience what Russell experienced and live through it. I am, at best, nonsurvivor-adjacent. Then there's the group's custom of introducing yourself by stating your relationship to the deceased and how this person died (my best friend, with the rope, in the barn). This, too, seems not meant for me. If you never shared a bed with the object of your grief, impostor syndrome sets in. For all this mandolining of loss, friendships are practically left out of the equation. This is the one type of relationship experienced by everyone on the planet, but when it comes to suicide? Friendship takes the backseat. Even when everyone was alive for it, my relationship with Russell did not exist in a tidy space. So why must it now? Why must friends be indirectly excluded from the conversation so that when inclusion comes, it feels like benevolence?

As I see it, there are two possible ways for me to digest what the world is telling me: The first is to "slip into suffering alone," chastising myself for wanting so much as an emoji from people whose spouses are gone. From people who found them gone. The second is to bypass the whole system. If these discussions aren't meant for me, then they don't apply to me. Does a not-as-bad loss equate to a not-as-bad death? Sure seems like it. Never mind that Russell *was* someone's partner, someone's son, someone's uncle, and someone's brother. He can't possibly be dead the way the Bot King's twins are dead . . . can he? These deaths seem unrelated and, according to the Internet, they kind of are. Thus, the fissure of fantasy opens even wider. "Almost impossible" sounds a lot like "anything's possible." I have my doubts about *sandwich bags* as a viable spirit medium, but with the jewelry, I have the Cadillac of conduits on my hands. So very nearly in my hands.

My first call is to the detective in the gray suit, with whom I share the eBay listings. The necklace is still at large but the tiger's-eye ring is en route to a friend's office. While it's safe to assume several degrees of separation between the man who broke into my home and the eBay seller, it's impossible to know how many. There's a big difference between someone who knows what they're looking at and someone who knew what they were looking for. The seller's wares include an assortment of designer handbags, candlesticks, and boxes of the morning-after pill. I am beyond interested in the person who traffics in this combination of goods. I would just prefer the interest not be mutual.

I don't expect Gray Suit to match my enthusiasm, but I do expect something akin to surprise. I have presented him with a lead on a burglary case with no fingerprints and no suspects.

There are two routes to solving a B&E: the possessions and the perpetrator. It is far more likely that the perpetrator will strike again than it is that your laptop will wash up on the banks of the Nile. Yet here I come, baby in a basket.

"There's nothing we can do," he tells me.

"Really?"

"We can subpoena eBay for the address of the account holder, but it may take a while. After that, we'd need probable cause."

I have heard of probable cause. I think we have it.

"We don't."

"Well, how do we get it?"

"Maybe if the ring comes with a note that says it's stolen."

His sense of justice and my sense of direction have this in common: I am happy to tell you how to get anywhere so long as you put me within ten feet of the destination.

"You can't knock on their door? *I* can knock on their door."

"It won't matter."

"Cool. But isn't it mail fraud, sending stolen goods?"

"You'd have to ask the post office."

"The post office has a justice system?"

I imagine them on horseback. Saddles of packing tape.

"Just keep me updated," he says.

"You keep me updated," I say.

"On what?"

My next call is to eBay's law enforcement department, which I imagine is in the same league, perhaps even the same softball league, as the Mail Mounties. The eBay law enforcement department is an electronics retrieval department. No serial number, no service. Their reasoning for this institutionalized apathy is that you can't just go around seizing property that happens to resemble yours. This seems like a far less likely scam than regular theft, yet the entire department is structured around the possibility of it. Perhaps, I suggest, there's a way to get more information without spooking the seller. They want to take the necklace down immediately and send the seller a note alerting them to a problematic listing. But I think we have time. No one is going to buy it in the next seventy-two hours. I just can't have it leaving that house.

My confidence stems from the one time I sold an item on eBay: a signed first edition of *The Da Vinci Code*. Every time I culled my bookshelves, I came across it, each time forgetting why I had it. Then I'd see it was signed and slide it back. While I was working at Vintage, Dan Brown stopped by the building to sign stock. Russell always encouraged his staff to seek out these signings because "you never know." I remember thinking this was uncharacteristically craven of him and I brought it up years later.

"I meant you never know if you'll like the author," he clarified. "Who wouldn't want to shake hands with Philip Roth? Why on earth would you go out of your way to meet Dan Brown?"

"Because you told me to."

"I really didn't."

"He was nice," I said. "I think he had on nice shoes."

"I should hope so."

By the time I decided to sell the book, the world had mostly recovered from the Judeo-Christian thriller craze. I got $70 for it and it took ages. I reason that if I had trouble unloading a signed first edition of one of the bestselling novels of the twenty-first century, we have a little time with a necklace priced like a used car.

"At least now we know you'll do anything I tell you to do," Russell had said, winking as I walked out of his office. "It's why I tell you all my secrets."

Object permanence applies to secrets too. Just because you aren't told information or don't want to hear it, doesn't mean it ceases to exist. And Russell loved his secrets. A subscriber to the pinkie swear, he'd appear on the threshold of my office, keeping his body pressed against the door as if holding an army of interested parties at bay. Then he'd launch into the world's most innocuous story. A woman in marketing had tried to ship a case of water to her apartment and it exploded in the mail room. Could I believe it?!

"Kind of?"

"Ugh," he'd groan, "you're no fun."

The information was never the point so much as his delight in sharing it. Book publishing is starved for proper scandal. You have to get your kicks somewhere. When information was truly damning, he said nothing or mentioned it so quickly, so casually, you'd have to grab him by the arm and say, "Wait, what?!"

Which is what happened the last night I saw him.

I am inclined to omit this part of the story from the story.

It's because I might, one day, be compelled to read these words out loud.

The day before our dinner, Russell and his partner had gotten into a fight. They tended to fight with the vigor of teenagers. I always marveled that, after so many years, they still cared enough to want to murder each other. Where I come from, all discontent is registered through a series of passive-aggressive barbs or by responding to a question that has been asked only once as if it's been asked fifty times in a row.

"What was the fight about?"

"What do you think it was about?"

Russell had begun putting his unhappiness where he had once put his happiness. He wasn't a hoarder per se, but he was engaging in a land grab for the past, for souvenirs of a more contented time. At first, it didn't seem like a problem. If you mentioned that you were in the market for an oil painting of a zebra, an hour later you were choosing from three. Looking for some tintype photos? By the box or by the pound? And the *books*. But the man worked in book publishing, what did we expect? Because I had not been to the house in some time, I was not there to watch things devolve. I was not there when he insisted on keeping old mattresses on the porch, promising he'd move them tomorrow. I was not there to witness the acquisition of gravy boats he already owned. I was not there when he agreed to throw away a rusted cocktail shaker but decided to hide it from his partner instead. Nor was I there for the subsequent discovery of the cocktail shaker.

The fight escalated quickly. Russell marched across the lawn, got into his car, and started the engine. His partner stopped him at the end of the driveway, knocking on the window, gesturing for him to roll it down.

"Whatever happens," his partner said, "don't kill yourself."

I was looking at the bill when Russell relayed this story.

He was sucking on a mint.

"What?" he asked, muffled by the mint.

"Why would he say something like that?"

"I don't know. Why does he do anything?"

"I guess I don't understand how you guys got from 'throw away this cocktail shaker' to 'don't kill yourself.'"

"Because he's crazy!"

It is often suggested that those left behind had an inkling of what was coming. *Did you know?* No one has the balls to ask us if we were given an inkling and didn't take it. If we ignored the signs when it counted, if we were too self-absorbed and neglectful. It's a haunting thought. But life cannot be lived like this, can it? Lunging at invisible monsters?

Sometimes I want to shake his partner and ask him why he didn't do more, if this was how they were talking. Why didn't he just cuff Russell to the nearest radiator and throw away the key? But I am a high-risk candidate for blame, that most misguided form of mourning. I'd begun practicing *before* Russell died. So much of the burglary is about blame. It's about looking for the bad guy, about the desire to have this person punished. Because, in the case of the burglary, there is a bad guy, there is a potential for restitution, and there is a potential for fairness. Not so for a suicide. So I aim the guilt closer to home. My friend was telling me something and I didn't listen. For how long had he been telling me?

The year prior, Russell iced his own birthday cake with the words "I'm Still Here," which everyone brushed off as a reference to the musical *Follies*. Because it is a reference to the musical *Follies*. But here is how that song is introduced:

> They thought it was a sad song but it kept on getting laughs. They told me to sing it sadder and so I did. I got out there and I gave them sad. And eighteen hundred people cracked up laughing.

When I want to defend myself to myself, I think this is the price of befriending a wit. If Fran Lebowitz said she'd rather kill herself than go to Times Square, would I ask her if maybe she should talk to someone? Not without full body armor, I wouldn't. So often we don't worry until there's nothing left to worry about. This is why people install alarm systems *after* they've been burglarized.

"Yeah, well," I said, sewing up the subject, "you're both completely out of your minds."

The guilt of this moment changes in diameter but never evaporates. To mourn the death of a friend is to feel as if you are walking around with a vase, knowing you have to set it down but nowhere is obvious. Others will assure you that there's no right way to do this. Put it anywhere. But you know better. You know that if you put your grief in a place that's too prominent or too hidden, you will take it back when no one's looking. This is why I spend my nights looking into the restaurant. I fantasize about keeping Russell in front of me for a little longer, asking him questions, knowing nothing either of us says will change the outcome. Each time the restaurant closes. Each time he drops me off at my door. Each time he walks off into the dark.

And then he's gone. And I am still holding this vase.

Around this time, when the only number I don't screen belongs to a vexed detective, I am given several self-help books on grief. I don't intend to read any of them, but somehow they all get read. I secretly hope they will be of more use than the philosophy, that I've been making things too cerebral. The books are certainly marketed for use and were purchased for use, recommended by meaningless algorithms to well-meaning consumers.

But taken as a lump, they present a familiar problem.

In *How to Go On Living When Someone You Love Dies*, the chapter titles are "Loss of a Spouse," "Loss of a Child," "Adult Loss of a Parent," "Adult Loss of a Sibling," and so forth. One chapter is called "What to Expect in Grief." When, I wonder, is one meant to purchase this book? Anyone who has experienced a sudden loss doesn't have a "before" to muck about in. The planning of funerals is a maudlin luxury. A sudden loss is not inherently worse than an expected one, but it is more likely to feel like it can be undone. It's the difference between forgetting your car keys at home and forgetting them on the driver's seat, where you can still see them. You're locked out either way.

How to Go On Living When Someone You Love Dies is a repetitive volume with nary a disagreeable sentiment, save the ones that are so sweeping, they become disagreeable. The book claims it was written because others were too flip, yet includes doozies such as: "Many losses are clearly perceived as unpleasant deprivations, such as the death of a child or the theft of valued jewelry."

Even I am not so far gone for such a pairing.

The Other Side of Sadness is a more elegant work, written by a scientist who unpacks our misconceptions about the grieving brain. Like its shelf-mates, it was written because "there is no shortage of books on grief and bereavement" but most "take a surprisingly narrow perspective." It is a truth universally acknowledged that every self-help book must come out of the gate by differentiating itself from every other self-help book until they all start to sound alike. It's unclear what they find so objectionable about one another. They are not Kant, no, but their intentions are pure. Some are informative. And none read: "Chapter One: Get Over It." The reason I can't get through *How to Go On Living When Someone You Love Dies* is not because it's useless. It's because it bounces off my temperament like a rubber ball.

Of all of them, *I Wasn't Ready to Say Goodbye* is my favorite. This is because it includes a one-page guide "for those helping others with grief," which is meant to be "photocopied and given to close friends and loved ones." The idea of wordlessly passing out a sheet of paper, preferably laminated, on *how to deal with me* provides me with the first laugh I've had in months. *I Wasn't Ready to Say Goodbye* reminds me of the titles of the eighties teen romance novels that Russell used to rescue from the giveaway shelf outside the office cafeteria and leave on my desk chair: *It's No Crush, I'm in Love!, He Noticed I'm Alive . . . and Other Hopeful Signs, I Will Go Barefoot All Summer for You, I'll Love You When You're More Like Me.*

My instinct to remove myself from the self-help books (help is for people whose loved ones are actually dead) or to write them off as schlock is curbed by how they begin:

"I remember all the vivid, surrealistic details of that morning . . ."

"April 1 was a beautiful, sunny day . . ."

Gradually, I start to understand why they are all so desperate to differentiate themselves and yet can't outright *trash* one another, why they are all so legibly diplomatic: It's because none of their authors have recovered. They want recovery and they want to be of use but if they have to pick? They'll take the recovery. Or, as a consolation prize, the catharsis. Alas, as the Italian author Natalia Ginzburg wrote, "You cannot hope to console yourself for your grief by writing. You cannot deceive yourself by hoping for caresses and lullabies from your vocation."

What you *can* do is be careful with other people. Human beings are solid things made out of delicate materials. Perhaps this is why we like jewelry as much as we do, because jewelry is our inverse—delicate things made out of solid materials. And it's not nice to poke too hard at someone else's open wound. Having written a book on loss yourself, who would know better than you how open that wound remains? Who would know better than you that the printed word should never be mistaken for the final word? Or that some part of you thinks that if you write the best story you can, he will hear you? Because what is the idea that something exists, even if you can't see it, if not the very definition of faith?

Good news: The tiger's-eye ring arrives safely, in a pod of bubble wrap. It feels cinematic, putting it on my finger, this souvenir from the past, tossed across the threshold. I ask it: *You have fun this time?* This isn't the ring's first escape attempt. Years ago, I was doing dishes in the kitchen of a man I was dating, washing up after dinner. I said: "Wanna see a terrible idea?" and slid the ring from my soapy finger, leaving it on the edge of his sink. Distracted by our breakup the next morning, I really did leave the ring. I had a friend pick it up for me, an immature errand that resulted in me peppering her with useless questions like "Did he seem sad?"

I flip my hand back and forth. You see? We *can* get back what we've lost. And, according to the return address, what we've lost is in Sheepshead Bay.

I go to my computer. The house is a split-level with aluminum siding, a stub of a driveway, and a family unit on each floor. There are no cars but there is a mailbox meant to look like an amphibian. I think perhaps the sender lives on the second floor because his eBay handle ends with a "2." Maybe I will go to this house and ring the buzzer. Perhaps I'll bring a friend, someone intimidating enough to act like a cop without actually being a cop. Perhaps flowers. Or a baseball bat. I make a list: flowers, bat, heavy.

I call a friend who used to be a PI and suggest that the two of us make a day of it, rent a van, get some sandwiches. I float the idea of gaining access to the house by asking to use the bathroom, a "my car broke down" plan divorced from both time (this isn't the fifties) and space (this is New York). He tells me that sounds like a terrible plan.

"What do you do when you're on a stakeout and you have to pee?"

"Gatorade bottles."

"Horrible."

"I don't do it anymore."

"Because of the pee thing?"

"No, not because of the pee thing."

My PI friend is too busy living his life or too uninterested in mine to come out of retirement, so he refers me to "some guys." If I want to go down this road. I very much do. The guys have a website detailing their careers as former Special Forces, former marines, former CIA, and former NYPD, but that's "all they can say." Seems to me they've said plenty. I doubt they'd work on a low-profile burglary case, but one of them calls me back, practically during the *whoosh* of my e-mail leaving my computer. He tells me he's in New Mexico so he can't talk long.

"Makes sense."

"I'm happy to wait outside their house," he says. "We know how to deal with this sort of element. The trick is to catch them doing it again."

I posit that selling items online would look a lot like a person typing.

"We know what we're looking for," he says, quoting me an outrageous sum.

I crowdsource more ideas, conduct polls. Here's a riddle: How do I get my necklace and keep it too? One idea is to buy the thing and claim it's fake. These people have no documentation. The cat was not giving out receipts. I like this plan, going as far as opening a PO box on Canal Street. But it's only half a plan. They'll just tell me to return it. Then what?

"Then you send them back a dead rat."

This comes from one of my male friends, who are fountains of atrocious ideas, every last one. Most of the time, I feel as if this crime happened to me, specifically, and not a woman, in general,

but when we start talking like this, our genders become pro-
nounced. My female friends find the idea of provoking criminals
who may or may not know where I live to be ill-advised.

"Where would I get a dead rat?" I ask.

"It's New York."

"Then *you* get a dead rat."

Another male friend suggests I send back an empty box ("Like
Gwyneth Paltrow's head but without the head," he clarifies) and
fight for the money in the courts of PayPal and American Express.
Another suggests cyberwarfare. He knows a guy who knows a guy
(where, oh where, have all the lady fixers gone?) who could freeze
his accounts, sign him up for jury duty, make his life a misery.
Have these men seen too many movies or too few?

Finally, I call Gray Suit with an imperfect idea of my own.
What if I buy the necklace, walk it over to the police precinct, and
hand it to him? Apparently, if you suspect you have purchased
stolen goods, you can relinquish them to police custody while the
cops track down the rightful owner. This should not take long.

"We can't do that."

"Oh, come *on*."

He is so loath to detect, I bet he winces at the sight of his own
business cards.

"We can't take responsibility for it."

"No, of course not."

"And unless you can prove it's stolen—"

"But I *can* prove it. We can prove it. The photos. The police
report."

"—we'd have it at the station forever. These things can take a
year to process."

"You have that many stolen necklaces?"

"I wouldn't know," he says, "I've never looked."

I wish Russell were here. He would tell me this will all work out. He always had a catlike view of his younger friends, particularly of the assistants who, even if they were not *his* assistant, he adopted as if they were. Whenever one of us would worry, he'd assure us we'd be fine. We'd land on our feet, and if we didn't, someone would be there to catch us because we were all so goddamn lovable. *He's trash. She's bitter. It's their loss they didn't hire you. You'll find a better apartment. Why? Because you're you.* Only in later years did I begin to hear these compliments as dismissive, shorthand implications that none of us knew from difficult. *What do you have to worry about? You're so clever, so young, so wanted.* These were the adjectives he thought no longer applied to him.

Bad news: The next time I click on the necklace, the link is dead.

Rather than revisit this pitiable scene (the rubbing of the temples, the screaming of the epithets, the defibrillation of the useless link), let us take this time to ask ourselves what we mean when we say "bring him back." Because it does not sound sane. On the slim chance I manage to locate the necklace a *second* time, I do not think that Russell will appear like a genie when I rub on the amber, a hologram spinning up from the core. Nor do I think he will reconstitute himself, his spirit returning to roam the earth. Though it would not be unheard of if I did think these things.

Countless burial rituals treat objects not as offerings but as gateways. Certain Native American cultures were known to burn the possessions of the deceased so that their spirits would not return through them. The Egyptians and Greeks were notorious for placing valuables within arm's reach of the dead. Across the board, the idea was that these people might come back for their shit, so let us not compound their stress with panic. According to civilizations with far longer histories than ours, you kinda *can* take it with you when you go. To the agnostic, there's something quaint about this line of thinking, especially when watered down by the secular centuries. We don't bury Grandpa with his watch because we think he'll need to tell time. There are no coins on contemporary eyes.

It's less socially acceptable to think the door swings both ways. But I have absorbed the ideas propagated by our current civilization and a bargain has been struck: In exchange for such an unbalanced death, what I get is a more permeable loss. A more debatable loss. Russell is his own murderer, sure, but his murderer will never be caught. Or—hold on—was he caught but never given a trial? Can we prove motive? Shall we unpack the word *manslaughter* or are we going to give ourselves a nosebleed? Even the two words *committed suicide* are debatable. Rather, they are offensive for obvious reasons. In 2015 (so maybe not so obvious), *The Associated Press Stylebook* began recommending "died by suicide" instead. But I find the secondary meaning of "committed" just as problematic. It casts the living as jilted brides, unchosen in favor of darkness.

Shortly after Russell died, the poet and critic A. Alvarez died, and I picked up his acclaimed study of suicide, *The Savage God*. For years, I'd meant to read it, mostly because of its focus on his relationship with Sylvia Plath, but also because it was already on my shelves. A barbaric scene near the beginning of the book sticks with me. Alvarez recounts the story of a man in nineteenth-century London who'd tried to kill himself by slitting his own throat. It didn't work so "they hanged him for suicide." Here, Alvarez is quoting the British historian E. H. Carr's *The Romantic Exiles*, a book about the Russian writer Alexander Herzen, which is itself quoting a letter from one of Herzen's appalled friends, who never saw the hanging but read about it in a newspaper. The context of the story keeps changing, but the description remains potent. It is not something I would recommend anyone read. And yet, in my current state, I am far less haunted by the grisly visuals than by the *choice* that was taken away from this man.

"There are always special reasons why a man should choose to die in one way rather than in another," writes Alvarez. I find the specific method of Russell's death, the method he chose (it would not have occurred to him to obtain or use a gun), has equally specific psychological effects. With gas or pills, I think, there's space. Time for the murderer to take one shape and the victim to take another, two versions of the same person, one who conceivably did not mean it. One who might have lived, for a short while anyway, to express self-condolences before sinking into oblivion. None of us is the exact same person we were an hour ago. In my grief-addled brain, I become obsessed with this idea and start thinking other *kinds* of suicide would have made for a "better" mourning process. This is the insensitive thought of someone whose only desire is for any story but the one she got. That doesn't stop me from having it.

The lack of time between the decision and the act, between the act and its consequence, makes it impossible to wish ill or peace upon Russell without feeling like I'm cutting the wrong wire. "Dying / Is an art, like everything else," wrote Plath, whose lifelong flirtation with death went too far one fateful February morning. And art is nothing if not subjective. In the same vein, when I think of Virginia Woolf, it is not merely as a helpless participant in the morbid fascination that has sprung up around these two writers—but of the windows of time of their deaths. The time it took Woolf to fill her pockets with rocks. The selection of those rocks. When does a suicide begin? When do we start counting? At the riverbank or in the river? In the kitchen the night before or the next morning? Rilke warned that "we must learn to die: That is all of life. To prepare gradually the master-piece of a proud and supreme death, of a death where chance plays no part, of a well-made, beatific, and enthusiastic death of the kind the saints knew to shape."

That's nice. But it's hard to throw something like that to-gether at the last minute.

What gruesome work suicide makes of grief! Sometimes I conflate blame and action, sometimes I separate them as if in a moral centrifuge, sometimes I think it doesn't matter either way.

Into all this comes the necklace. I am wedging this piece of fossilized tree sap into the chaos. That will stop the wheel from turning. There is no logic at work beyond that. During this time, I believe, as much as I believe in my own reflection, that Russell will know the necklace is in my possession. And then what? It wasn't his stupid necklace. It wasn't even his favorite. But my brain cannot be bothered with pedestrian questions like "how" or "why." It knows only "must." It knows only that it must stop the bleed. If the necklace can come home, then everything will be just as it used to be.

I scour the Internet. Wake up, scour. Eat lunch, scour. Go to bed, scour. Shower, no scour. I imagine a tagline for a superhero sequel: *This time, it's personal.* Like it wasn't personal before? Two whole months pass this way. Looks like I *do* have a hobby after all—searching for the necklace is my sole leisure activity. The not finding starts to feel productive. It doesn't matter how many amber necklaces there are in the world or how many lifetimes it would take just to look at them all, there is gratification in the process of elimination. Every day is an opportunity to confirm where the necklace is not. The necklace is not on Craigslist. The necklace is not at the corner deli. The necklace is not in this cereal box. Having located the thing and lost it again sometimes fills me with the fear I'll never get another chance. Other times, it fills me with the confidence that I will. These feelings cancel each other out until all that's left is the brightness of screens.

Perhaps this is why, on the evening of December 27, 2019, exactly six months after the burglary, when the necklace appears on a new seller's page, I feel neither shock nor relief. Only determination: *So we meet again, my carrot-colored friend.* This time, there will be no cops, no plaintive e-mail to eBay, no bureaucracy.

I will not be at the mercy of the system. This time, I am a vigilante, Queen of the Underground.

This time, it's personal.

The new seller is in Manhattan. The necklace is getting closer. Unfortunately, this seller has a more impressive inventory than the previous one. There are diamond tennis bracelets and engagement rings that smack of a challenging extrication process. But the photographs are the same, having been passed from one criminal to another. I can sense this network of thieves, rustling like creatures in the wall. When I tell my mother about finding the necklace again, she is quiet for a long time. Then she says: "I might remind you that we didn't *like* my mother."

I hang up the phone. I don't have time for this lack of vision.

As I examine this new seller's wares, getting the lay of the land, one item stands out: a vintage Rolex. I click on it, tapping through photos of the bezel, zooming in on the little dials. I whisper: "Wanna help me spring a necklace?"

It's been ages since I've spoken to the man on whose kitchen sink I left my ring, but I remember this much: He collects vintage Rolexes. Sometimes this is as rarefied a prospect as it sounds, sometimes it can be done on eBay. Most of the men I've dated are not in possession of a design sensibility that could be confused for intent, but this one has a real wardrobe. Because his eBay profile shows a history of purchasing big-ticket items, I reason it will not be suspicious when he wins an auction for a watch he has absolutely no intention of purchasing. It will not be suspicious when he then asks the seller if he can examine the watch before transferring the money, thereby procuring the address where my necklace is being kept. It's a flawless plan.

"Why don't I just bid directly on the necklace?"

"*Because*," I say, rolling my eyes, "the necklace has a ton of heat on it."

"You're unwell."

"Yeah? You weren't here for the rats."

He is keen to help. On top of being a generous person, a heist triggers his hero complex. So he hatches an even more involved plan. Once he has the address, he will arrange a watch-viewing appointment, during which he will find a scratch in the face. Too bad. But maybe he can buy a gift for his girlfriend while he's here? He will then grab the necklace, brandish a copy of my police report, and say something along the lines of "You don't want any trouble here."

"You can't do that."

"You don't want to risk losing five grand on this deal, do you?"

Hey now. King of the Underground.

For a while, all our plans are moot. The seller is oddly evasive about the watch, even with a firm offer on the table. Do we reek of a sting operation, of people who have, only very recently, become hard-boiled pulp fiction characters? The seller is constantly out of town or busy. Only after weeks of judicious follow-ups does he fork over a time (3:00 p.m.), a date (tomorrow), and an address: West Forty-seventh Street. The heart of the diamond district.

When I saw the price tag for the necklace on the first seller's page, there was a sense of relief embedded in my outrage. The necklace's value is not obvious to the untrained eye. But as one of the higher-priced items on the first seller's page, at least whoever wound up with it would know not to pick her teeth with it. Now that it's been transferred to the largest diamond market in the world, its fate feels less certain. It's in flattering company but it's no prize pig. These people could move it without missing it. We need to get it out of there.

So I agree to my ex's plan.

He texts me a few minutes before his appointed viewing time to tell me he's headed into the building. In response, I share a photograph of Obama in the situation room, watching the Navy SEALs raid Bin Laden's home. I pace in my apartment, which I do not realize I'm doing until I smash my toe on a stool. The cat darts out of the room. Ten minutes later, the phone rings.

"Abort," he says.

"What happened?!"

He starts whispering as if he were still inside even though he's out on the street. Nothing has happened. That's the problem. The place is "beyond shady," a closet of a room above street level with a man and a woman guarding a safe.

"And I couldn't exactly be like, 'What's in the safe?'"

"Right, right."

As the writer David Rakoff once observed, "There are some questions in life, the very speaking of which are their own undoing. Am I fired? Is this a date? Are you breaking up with me?" I would add "What's in the safe?" to that list.

"And they wouldn't let me see the watch. I showed them my exchange with the guy. They said they had no idea what I was talking about."

"Really? What are you wearing?"

"What's that got to do with anything?"

"Are you maybe wearing more than one polo shirt at the same time?"

"Screw you, Nancy Drew."

I have limped myself into the bedroom and am sitting on the bed, watching the empty spice cabinet. I have been given so much from other people. Here, have this booze, this soup, these condolence cards, these books, this friendship. Have this help from people you used to know. Have a room in a house upstate for the weekend and a standing dinner invitation and a weighted blanket. Have this ring a friend's daughter made out of pipe cleaners. Have a case number for the police and a prescription from the doctor and a log-in for a grief group. The world is built for no one, not even a Sedgwick, but right now it is built for you. Why is none of it enough?

Because I got left. That's why.

"I'm going in," I tell my ex.

"You can't do that. What if they shoot you?"

"No one's going to *shoot* me," I say, 98.4 percent sure of it.

The amber pendant is the same color as these subway seats. There's a woman across from me in a moth-eaten coat, carting around a caddy of dog food. We smile at each other. It's unpredictable, this stage of grief. Just when you think you have a handle on it, a crack opens up where the crazy gets in. The pain is a weather system that builds and expands, occasionally touching down, like lightning. If you have ever thrown your back out while brushing your teeth, you're familiar with the sensation. There were a thousand movements that contributed to this injury, but technically? You threw your back out because you spat in a sink.

When I exit the station, I walk the wrong way down Forty-seventh Street, clocking the ascending numbers but moving backward. I am so nervous, I have forgotten how counting works. This does not bode well for my negotiation skills. I wonder: Is this a stupid thing I'm doing or an immensely stupid thing I'm doing? My desire to rescue a piece of the past is obscuring an unknown percentage of my common sense. Even if I did want to turn back, I clearly can't be trusted to go in the right direction.

The building's entrance is wedged between two storefronts that put one in mind of fish tanks. Men in black gabardine mill about on the other side of glass displays. This jewelry calls out to a conception of beauty that runs parallel to my own. The lighting and the diamonds have a perfect marriage in that the structure of one is designed with the other in mind. In theory, I should like it. I examine the buzzer panel, the plastic buttons better suited for an apartment building.

"Just push the handle," offers a security guard wearing a beanie with an NYPD patch sewn like a target on his forehead.

He belongs to one of the fish tank stores. Manning this door with no names is a geographical by-product of his day. I find his tone assuring. If other people come here often enough to warrant exasperation, it means they also come out.

Once inside, I am confronted with a poster for "kosher delights" hanging in the stairwell, advertising the restaurant on the top floor with a photograph of a giant kebab. There's a poster at each landing, like a scavenger hunt for lamb. But there is no whiff of a restaurant. I go to the top floor and poke my head in. It's lunchtime but the chairs are flipped over. There's a buffet station, covered in plastic, dusty cartons of plastic cups, and a back door with multiple padlocks. A restaurant seems like a tedious criminal front. I don't know *what* these people are doing but they're not selling family heirlooms out of broom closets.

My destination is suite 303. The number is written in the jaunty penmanship of someone who taped the paper to the door first and wrote on it second. There are multiple entrances embedded in two-way mirrors. I press one of the buzzers and stand beneath a camera so it can get a clear shot of me, of my harmless demeanor, my empty hands. I press again. No answer. Then a door to my right opens and I dart toward it. Two bearded men are on their way out. They look at me as if I am an uncategorizable species of person.

The room is just as my ex described it. It has the oppressive brightness of a car rental kiosk. There's a Formica floor and four windowless walls, one with a wall calendar, still stuck on a photograph of a menorah. But the head count is a little different. There are not two people in this room. There are ten men. Four are sitting on folding chairs, two are standing on one side of a partition, two of them on the other side, a tall one is leaning against the safe in the back, and an elderly Hasidic gentlemen is asleep on a peeling La-Z-Boy, the only furniture in the room. The two men on the other side of the partition are outfitted in velour tracksuits, a hint of gold at their necks. The door clicks shut behind me.

"Who sent you?" demands one of the men on the other side of the partition.

I have never heard anyone ask this question in real life.

"No one sent me," I say, testing the sound of my own voice. "I was hoping to speak with the manager."

"Fourth floor," he says with a dismissive lack of eye contact.

"Not the restaurant," I say, trying to act knowing. "I was wondering about this store."

"It's not a store."

He laughs and gestures at our surroundings like I must be some kind of idiot. He would, quite transparently, like me to leave. This must be the same man who wouldn't let my ex see the watch. I had convinced us both that it was okay for me to come alone, that we were underestimating the power of the lost lamb here. But if no one takes pity on me, there are a number of viable reactions to my presence. I fear mockery more than violence. But I fear it just the same.

I smirk, aiming somewhere between escalation and inertia. I'm recording this conversation for nebulous purposes and there's five hundred dollars in cash spread across my body, some of it heating up at the bottom of my shoes. But these don't look like shoe-cash people. There's a flat-screen television in the corner, tuned to a PBS documentary.

I try to imagine what Russell would do. At the flea market, on the rare occasions he could not persuade a vendor to lower their price, he'd unhand the conversation and walk away. Then he'd double back and chitchat, recounting his morning, asking the vendor about theirs, sharing the stories of his other purchases. Next thing you know, he was wrapping a cord around the art deco lamp of his dreams. So I do as he would have done. I inform the group that I have a story to tell them. It will take five minutes and everyone is welcome to stay for it. The elderly gentleman in the La-Z-Boy rouses, surveying the room, stopping at me, blinking. I hand a copy of the photograph and the eBay listing to the man who is now leaning forward on the partition, arms straight, shoulders raised.

"Visual aids?" he asks, his accent recasting it as "odds."

This time, everyone laughs. I laugh too, trying to pry open this crack of bemusement, but it shuts as quickly as it opened. He is expressionless as he studies the images. What is there to study, I do not know, but this is the same face I make when trying frozen yogurt samples at an airport. *And what is this concoction you call "mint chocolate chip"? What might that be like?* Perhaps he is weighing the benefits of admitting he has the necklace, assessing the likelihood that I am a PI. Do I smell like piss and Gatorade?

The PBS documentary is about a woman who escaped Iran with her son. This makes for unfortunate background noise as I tell my tale of comparatively minor woe. I start with the boot prints on my bed. I tell them the thief took my grandmother's Jewish star "from the war" (I am missing a Jewish star "from the nineties"). Then I tell them how I intended to rip them off, about the Egg and Gray Suit and the pawnbrokers and the dead rats. And now we have come to the end. If they like, they can pretend they have never laid eyes on the necklace. It will be like none of this ever happened. Because I have nothing left. No more leads. I have given my sanity to the past, my heart to Russell, and my leverage to these strangers. If all that happens after today is that they have looked me in the eye, *dayenu*.

They whisper to one another in Hebrew. This is overkill. One or the other will do.

Finally, the tall man by the safe speaks:

"Where would you get a dead rat?"

"*Thank you.*"

"They broke into your house?" the elderly gentleman in the La-Z-Boy pipes in.

He has a Long Island drawl, like stones skipping over the East River.

"Yes."

"In Manhattan?"

Men-hat-tin.

"Yes."

"A shame," he tsk-tsks.

Ten centuries of religious persecution have prepped this person for bad things. I'm sure he'd have a similar reaction to a suicide. A *shonda*, what's for lunch?

"This one," says the man with my photos, tapping the image of the necklace, "I know this one. Tomorrow you'll come back and we can have a discussion."

I look at the safe.

"Can we have a discussion today?" I ask, trying to level my tone.

"It's not here right now."

It's possible he's telling the truth. But I am quite familiar with his merchandise and it's all compact. Where else would the necklace be if not the safe?

"Tomorrow," he repeats. "Ask for Dimitri. I am Dimitri."

"Okay," I say. "Thank you."

I have caught him off guard. Perhaps he will be better prepared tomorrow. I have a lot of nerve, waltzing in here, making accusations. He's a businessman. Do I have any idea who I'm dealing with?

Not really, no.

My liquor store does not have a ton of kosher wine options so I use the traditional method and pick the second-cheapest bottle. As I walk down Forty-seventh Street, paper bag tied with a flammable ribbon, I nod at the security guard in the beanie. I have more cash on my person than I did yesterday. Some of it is in my bra, which feels like a mistake. Regardless, I don't know how these negotiations will shake out. If I bring too little, my search will have been for naught. If I bring too much, I might give away too much. I don't want to spend years calculating all the things I'm not paying for to justify buying back my own necklace.

Yesterday, I spotted cameras in the stairwell. So I have returned alone. I don't want anyone thinking I brought backup. Hard-boiled or not, it delights me to think this way, to feel at home in this space of transaction and darkness, in this land where the only law is the law of what you can get away with. Did Russell know a version of this world? Multiple versions? Multiple secrets? Suicide, unlike most deaths, is math you work backward instead of forward. It's enough to make you crazy.

In the halogen light of a new day, suite 303 seems somewhat defanged. Today's cast of characters is limited to Dimitri, a woman in a sheer frilly blouse, and a man in a leather bomber jacket who, like myself, has business here. I hang back as Dimitri and this man have an exchange involving an envelope and a hug. They pat each other's backs. After the man leaves, Dimitri starts speaking to the woman in Hebrew but she interrupts him, nodding at me.

"Oh," he says, upon seeing my face, "is this for me?"

"It is," I say, instantly embarrassed by the wine.

I place the bag on the partition, which is narrower than the base of the bottle. The woman watches me perform this balancing act without interfering. She remains unimpressed. Meanwhile, Dimitri is patting at his pockets and lifting papers, as if having misplaced his glasses. At long last, he removes an object from the top of the safe.

It's a plastic sandwich bag.

My eyes widen at the sound of the necklace being extracted from the bag. When Dimitri turns around, he is holding the amulet by its chain. The silver has begun to oxidize around the amber. If you wear silver every day, you will never have to polish it. The grease of life keeps it gleaming.

"Give me your hand," he instructs, which I do, obediently.

He drops the necklace in my palm, dripping the chain on top of itself.

Then he closes my fingers for me and says: "Take it. That shouldn't have happened."

What the fuck, I wonder, *should* have happened? But I am distracted by how lightweight it is. Every time I looked at a photograph of the necklace, it gained an ounce.

"What happened to you was not right," he emphasizes. "Just take it."

I feel the sting of tears in my eyes.

"Are you *crying?*"

I shake my head. Everyone from the closest of friends to the most distant of eBay operators has approached the story with a baseline construct of "shit happens." It's the same with the suicide. Is it awful? Yes. Is it unheard of? No. That's part of the awfulness. Most bad things exist within the same brutal reality. But Dimitri's reality is a little different. Here is a person who spends his time at the murky end of the morality spectrum. This gives him the authority to assess crimes for what they are, not for what they feel like. Life is unfair, sure, but it's not this unfair. I shouldn't walk around thinking it's this unfair.

"Anything else?" asks the woman in the frilly blouse, hand on her hip.

Clearly, a debate has been had as to how best to proceed with this situation and she has lost. This is why Dimitri couldn't give me the necklace yesterday—because she wasn't here to approve it.

I am unable to pry my fingers off the amber. We'll be home soon and I'll look at it when we're safe. Alas, my plan will not work. Everything will not be just as it used to be, not ever again. I tried to bargain my way backward through time because I thought that if I could, at least one of us could remain unchanged by what happened. That's what Russell would've wanted. It's what he wanted when he was alive, for me to stay trapped in amber forever. *What do you have to worry about? You have all the time in the world.* I put up a good fight. But it's time to stop fighting now. I am older than I used to be and Russell is dead in the same way everyone who has ever died is dead.

Still, I have managed to preserve a small piece of faith as a souvenir. Whatever the contours of death, perhaps they're porous

enough that the dead have the capacity to know, whatever knowing means to them, what occurred soon after they died. And they
are not shocked by any of it because in death, all knowledge is the
same. Everything you learn, you already knew, everything you
know you have yet to learn. Perhaps, in this one object, the past
will have a bridge to the present, a bridge that will join wherever
Russell is to wherever I am until the day, a long time from now,
when we can meet in the middle.

The woman in the frilly blouse clears her throat. I can see
her bra.

"Are we done?" she asks, meaning: "Take your free jewelry
and go."

"Yes," I croak, turning to leave.

"And another thing!" Dimitri shouts a little too loudly, as if
he's in the middle of a rant. "If you ever want to sell it, you know
where to find me."

Then he winks and buzzes me out the door.

PART III

KIDS OF ALL AGES

(ANGER)

ACT 1: SHANGRI-LA
ACT 2: PURGATORY
ACT 3: THE DESCENT

ACT 1: SHANGRI-LA

There was no daylight between our professional and personal lives and we did not see how this could turn into a problem. The house in Connecticut had morphed into a home for wayward literary youth. Weekends were idyllic scenes, the porch strewn with disemboweled newspapers, overflowing ashtrays, strings of corn silk, plates of half-eaten toast, and every member of our department conked out on wicker sofas as two huskies took turns digging their claws into our thighs. During the day, we'd read or swim or cheat at lawn games. Down by the pond, the frogs spent their evenings mating. After dark, the strings of paper lanterns came on and I'd volunteer to retrieve forgotten items from the pool house. I cherished the view on the way back, the dip and glow of the lights. The only real eyesore was the barn, a derelict structure with holes in the roof. I never went into the barn. I cannot conjure the inside of the barn.

From 2002 to 2010, we lived in a Terrence McNally play by way of Metro-North. We talked into the night, our bellies full of meals prepared by Russell's partner: tomato bruschetta, vegetable terrines, baked salmon, cheesecake surrounded by a fort of crust. We smoked weed and listened to Etta James and watched *The Boys in the Band*. We gossiped, presenting one another with third-party infractions and coming down on the desired side. Russell was forever pitching us his favorite subgenre of literature: Old Hollywood. *Picture* by Lillian Ross, *What Makes Sammy Run?* by Budd Schulberg, *Monster* by John Gregory Dunne. He longed for a time when glamour was glamorous, when scandals were worth the trouble, when Grace Kelly wore pearls to bed. When the gods behaved badly but at least they were gods. Russell took me to see a documentary about Scotty Bowers, a WWII veteran who became a prostitute and procurer to Los Angeles's closeted movie stars. He liked stories about people who had been there all along. I was familiar with the material, having read Bowers's memoir in Russell's hammock, drifting off to sleep behind a mound of hydrangeas.

We were so spoiled. These men provided us with an escape from New York at an age when we didn't really need it. The decision to brave the pool after the hot tub was not a good problem to have in comparison with our actual problems because we didn't have actual problems. Not yet. The crash had yet to come. Our parents were still in good health. Our student debt had yet to pile up. Our roommates were reasonably sane. We hadn't wounded one another too badly. Life in Connecticut was a taste of our collective inevitability, as if we were trying on a future with no sense that we might one day have to give it back. Or, as an old colleague once put it: It was not the number of years we spent up there but the years they were. Even when someone told a hurtful joke or broke a dish or was ordered to leave the room because she's so bad at cards, she's lucky she doesn't get fired for being an imbecile, joy was the dominant twin. It absorbed everything.

Our contemporaries spent their Saturday nights packed onto tar roofs or crowded into expensive clubs, but we let ourselves off the hook, waking up on Sunday mornings with virgin wrists. Turns out you're never too young to feel relieved about not having to shave your legs. Sometimes I went up to the house on my own, to write, to lie in the grass, or to get some perspective if I was, as Russell liked to put it, "down in the dumps."

My room was mine even when I was nowhere near it. *We got a new dresser for your room. We found two ladybugs going at it on your pillow. We heard a noise and I said, "I think it's coming from Sloane's room."* The walls were covered in yellow wallpaper with splotchy flowers. Over those were nailed panoramic photos of banquet hall events, all purchased by Russell at the flea market. The room was tiny, airless, and impossible to sleep in, especially with more than one person. Any male guests of mine would wake on the porch, having migrated there in defeat. By the time I came downstairs, Russell would've gotten to them, poking at their professional histories, testing their worthiness via Sondheim lyrics. Later, I would be told with the hushed enthusiasm of a Jewish mother that a gentleman was a "keeper" or, with the withering verdict of a Protestant mother, that he was "interesting."

"Country house in Connecticut" has gleaming associations: crisp duvet covers, citrus centerpieces, linen sofas with no moth holes in them. Russell's partner, who worked from home and gravitated toward minimalist spaces, would have preferred a closer alignment between conception and reality. But theirs was a modest farmhouse with peeling paint and fragile plumbing, and there was no keeping Russell's collecting at bay. No stopping the influx of pillboxes and platters, of gadgets that had to be turned right side up in my hands. This was the house that Windex forgot. At night, I'd mainline Benadryl while a fan shook its head at my efforts. Eventually, I'd turn on the bedside lamp and read one of the copies of *Here at The New Yorker* that seemed to breed behind our backs. Or else I'd stare at the banquet hall photos, resting my gaze on a woman in a feathered hat. What had she been talking about before she'd been instructed to smile? Had Russell noticed her too? I never got the chance to ask.

Russell never told me he loved me. He told other people he loved me. I suppose there's a possibility he said it in passing, a drunken farewell tossed over a turnstile, and I missed it. But I don't recall him using the words, even in the conformational way people do when their friends behave in a manner that's quintessentially *them*. Russell could not stomach sadness but he could not stomach earnestness either.

When I dedicated my third book of essays to him, I held off on showing him the galley until we were sitting across from each other at a diner booth. So he couldn't escape. What did I want, to force him to tell me what I already knew? Who is a book's dedication for anyway? In the Barbara Pym novel *Excellent Women*, a character decides that an unsolicited declaration of love must be "something like a large white rabbit thrust into your arms and not knowing what to do with it." If there is a better description of Russell's reaction, I don't know it. He seemed almost angry as he thanked me, rattling off a list of people who would've made better candidates. It wasn't too late for me to change it.

"Why me?"

"Don't get a big head," I assured him, smiling, "it's just essays."

"But I didn't do anything."

"You did everything."

"I just can't believe you did that."

"Well, I love you."

"That's nice but you shouldn't have done that."

"You're *welcome*," I said, pouring milk into my coffee to stop it from steaming.

Like I wanted to shut it up.

"It's intolerable being tolerated." That's from *A Little Night Music*. Someone needed to get this man some Gershwin.

We had moved from a place of me making Russell feel comfortable, of trying to tourniquet his reflexive self-erasure, to one of him making me feel ashamed. I should have closer friends by now. Or more literary ones. I could sense it: I had been an author, and an author only, for long enough. My thoughts should not be with those behind the scenes, with the workhorses and the giving trees. There was no place for me on the factory floor. *Shoo, shoo.* He shoved the galley into his messenger bag.

Apparently, the next morning, he went around the office, showing it to everyone as they came in. He flipped open the cover, beaming from doorway to doorway, before returning it to its permanent home, beneath the note from the woman he'd once called "unfun." He'd point to it in the same way. As evidence. *Talk to the dedication.*

By the time I presented him with the book, in early 2018, I had not been invited up to the house in nearly a decade. Not only had I not been invited, I'd run out of ways to invite myself. At first, I was told I was welcome anytime. My room was still mine. But when I picked weekends, they were never the right weekends. The kitchen was being redone, the floors sanded, the pool filled with packing peanuts. Or his partner was "being funny" about guests. One time the chicken coop was being torn down, a piece of information presented to me as if I'd be sleeping there. If I knew a little something about why this was happening then, I know even less now.

What I do know: In the summer of 2005, our bucolic bubble began to dissolve because of some kind of affair that occurred between one of us and Russell's partner. I don't know if the affair was ever physical, but I certainly witnessed the emotional half of it. When Russell's partner turned fifty, our friend presented him with a blank journal that he passed around like a yearbook. Our friend filled three pages with tiny cursive, private jokes curling up the margins. I took up half a page. Russell wrote: "Happy Birthday!"

Our friend was a charming Southern boy who looked like a

draft of Rob Lowe. Russell's partner was a kind, introspective man with a fraught family history. He'd also lived in San Diego and Los Angeles during the eighties, where he'd seen half of his friends die from AIDS. Trauma had become his love language. He liked finding people's wounds, excavating them, holding them up to the light and examining them with the kind of careful consideration Russell applied to my dome ring. Frailties that were in danger of being crushed by Russell were more likely to be cradled by his partner. Whenever I invited my own guests, I'd issue a quick warning as we pulled into the train station or rolled up the driveway: *By the way, you won't make it through this weekend without crying about your mother. Shall we?*

In retrospect, there was an undercurrent of procurement to this time period, to Russell bringing up so many of us and so often. He heedlessly encouraged the kind of unstructured company retreat that could never happen now (I have memories of refereeing naked pool-noodle fights, of Russell flinging open my door at dawn, demanding to know why I wasn't dressed yet). He was pathologically social and abrasively generous—God help you if he discovered you'd made it three days without asking for an extra towel—but he also wanted to create a group. It just worked a little too well.

So many flirtations passed under my nose while I was busy musing about ladies in feathered hats. Our young friend became possessive over Russell's partner, asserting his closeness. They had a connection, we had to understand. He seemed anointed by the attention of someone from America's actual lost generation, and offered an endless supply of interest in return. Except it wasn't quite endless. Russell would only tell me that the affair nearly destroyed the marriage, not because he felt betrayed (Russell had his own extracurricular activities—this is someone who never saw the point in leaving the flea market with one dog toy when there were twenty to be had), but because our friend had "grossly misrepresented" himself. When things turned sour, he disappeared, popping up again only to "aggressively pursue" friendships with the other gay couples he'd met through them. This was the Devil Himself we were dealing with and I was never to speak this person's name again. Russell had invited a fox into the henhouse. The guilt radiated off him.

And he was notorious for tending to his grudges like babies in the ICU.

Now, I am fated to a partial assessment of events, as I was neither fully involved nor fully debriefed. But it's safe to say the Devil Himself is not a twenty-five-year-old book publicity assistant. Probably. The most generous assessment I can make is that our friend did not have the bandwidth to maintain a long-distance correspondence with someone else's husband, and once he got what he wanted, an indoctrination into an elusive part of his own history, he didn't exit with grace. But who knows? We were kids. The guy may or may not have patronized a men's clothing store called Wear Me Out, which is a triple, if not a quadruple, entendre.

Meanwhile, Russell's partner, also a registered nurse in the Grudge ICU, did the one thing everyone *wants* to do after a breakup but few *get* to do: burn the evidence. Heartbreak survivors will be familiar with this fantasy of nonexistence. Nonexistence is not vengeance. You simply want the offending party to go away, for your friends to never run into or mention them, for their neighborhood to be wiped off the map. Because Russell's partner came into the city on a voluntary basis, he had the option to do this. It happened slowly, taking a while for all of us to catch on, taking a while for everyone to make other summer plans. But Russell couldn't dodge me forever. Eventually, he admitted that, actually, no one was allowed up at the house. Not anymore. Not anyone who'd been associated with what happened.

There is no violin small enough for having a country house yanked out from under you. That wasn't the issue. The issue was that, once this policy became de rigueur, it expanded. At first, only their friends whose kids wanted to use the pool were allowed. Then just old friends. Then just blood relations. Then, according to Russell at least, only a couple of times a summer. Now the only videos Russell posted were of the dogs cooling off in the pool, keeping their tails afloat. Now the chicken coop really *was* being redone, but who, aside from its residents, was there to see it? Russell may have been the one responsible for making the place look like *Grey Gardens* but he was not the one who staged the reenactment.

At least, this is the version of the story we were fed. The version I was fed. But all stories have more than one entrance. The idea that Russell, the most outspoken personality to ever grace the streets of Litchfield County, could not override what was happening if he really wanted to, that he would allow his social oxygen to be cut off, is somewhat implausible. But whatever the cause, in those final years, none of us got through the gates.

Not even Brooke.

Around the time we were being pushed out, Russell and his partner became close with Brooke Hayward, who lived nearby. A famed actress and art scene doyenne in 1960s Los Angeles, as well as Dennis Hopper's ex-wife, Brooke was human catnip for Russell. There's not a single biographical detail I could share about Brooke that wouldn't be a gross understatement. Here was real Hollywood royalty, parking at the Stop & Shop. And she *adored* Russell. He even persuaded Vintage to reissue her 1977 memoir, *Haywire*. This was not a typical route for publication (*Dear Sir or Madam, my neighbor once went out with Warren Beatty, what are we going to do about it?*), but Russell's argument was strong and he was the one to make it. *Haywire* had been a number one *New York Times* bestseller and now it was an all-but-forgotten glimpse into the Golden Age. And, much like *Edie*, it was about a very rarified life gone very wrong.

Brooke was always giving him gifts from her home—tablecloths, nutcrackers, nesting bowls, candlesticks. A rusted cocktail shaker. She was unloading the past, he was collecting it: It was a match made in heaven. I read *Haywire* with a ridiculous twinge of jealousy for this eighty-year-old woman to whom Russell had taken such a shine. I could not compete with firsthand accounts of young Jane Fonda, Jimmy Stewart, Greta Garbo, or Slim Keith, whom Brooke's father married after he divorced her mother. I suspect Brooke, though only half aware of my existence, knew this. The one time I tagged along to her home, I was offered a chipped clay frog from a Goodwill box upon my departure.

Brooke became Russell and his partner's entire social life outside the city. For this, I am grateful. But I also wonder if the specter of suicide bonded them without either of them knowing it. Both of Brooke's siblings died by suicide, her sister with pills, her brother with a handgun. Her mother overdosed on barbiturates after a prolonged struggle with depression. Russell knew what Brooke had seen. Perhaps she knew, without *knowing*, what Russell wanted to see. Perhaps she recognized something nameless but familiar in him. In a way, didn't we all?

All that glamorizing of the past had seemed a piece of our Arcadian heaven. As much as we talked the way people do when they just want to eat half a blueberry cobbler and take a nap, those weekends were stealth art, literature, and film classes. What were the imitative elements of the novel or movie at hand? Who in the past had done it better or with more sincerity? *Hollywood movies used to just end and you didn't have to know everything.* Were we snobs? I have asked myself this many times, if Russell had begun thinking he was too good for everything, himself included. Perhaps his criteria for worth had grown so long, he'd bumped himself off the list. But it seems impossible that he, who had come from so little, and I, who had to put Lorrie Moore on hold whenever she called because I would've had more composure around the Easter Bunny, could be true snobs.

Russell's fascination with the dead was hiding in plain sight. Because he oversaw the paperback publicity campaigns, he was in charge of resurrecting literary lions, of keeping them alive in the press. He was the antiques dealer of the book world. At least he talked like it. He liked to speak of how one should be on the side of the bygone, otherwise people forget too easily, of how the dead, because they are dead, are more perfect. No one blinks at nihilism when it's disguised as good taste. It is only now that Russell is gone that I can see how poisonous such obsessions are for a person who makes the dead more alive than the living, a person in grave danger of joining their ranks. It is only now that I can see the dark spots in the sunlight—the sick tree rotting by the pond, the bloated possum floating in the pool, the lanterns that flickered and went dark.

Russell and his partner went out to dinner with Brooke on the evening of July 27, 2019. It was their Saturday ritual away from a house that had become cramped in more ways than one. Then Brooke went home. Then they went home.

Then only two of them woke up the next morning.

Nowadays, when Russell appears in my dreams, we're always having the best time. We're doubled over laughing, soaking chair cushions with our wet bathing suits. Or else he's flipping me out of the hammock and throwing me in the pool. Other times, we're back in the city, drinking whiskey in Midtown before heading to the opera to watch the chandeliers rise. He points up. *That looks like your grandmother's ring. Don't you think?* He stifles a giggle as the house lights dim. He had one of those laughs where you can really make out the "ha!" By the same token, whenever I can't sleep, I imagine myself in that airless room in Connecticut where I was never unconscious for more than an hour straight. Just the thought of it knocks me right out. Heavy is the enchantment of places you know you will never see again.

ACT 2: PURGATORY

In "Goodbye to All That," Joan Didion writes, "It is easy to see the beginnings of things, and harder to see the ends." When it comes to our personal life, this resonates. I remember every detail of my first weekend in Connecticut but not of my last because I didn't know it would be my last. But when I consider how Russell's professional happiness crumbled, when it started to turn into anger, I'm not sure I can see either. Perhaps this is because where I began is not the beginning. The generation behind me is nostalgic for an institutional ease of which I can barely conceive, which, for all its systemic flaws, was safe from the ruinous interferences of technology. I witnessed the tail end of it, before the battle royale between the robots and the dinosaurs began in earnest. I imagine every industry is like this. Maybe the people behind you had it better and maybe they had it worse, but it always feels like they knew what the hell was going on.

This is why I am dubious of New York stories in general. As a reader, the parade of proper nouns is lovely, like hearing your name in a song. But it's a rickety enterprise that rests on the assumption that your tale is worth telling by virtue of where it took place. All those bars and street corners (*We lived on Delancey then . . .*) are just as liable to push readers away as to invite them in. The only reason they don't is because the author has used the city to make average tales appear wild. There is, however, one constant I admire in other people's accounts of New York, and that is the confidence with which they pinpoint change. There's always that moment when life turned from solid to liquid: One day the subway required tokens, the next it didn't. One day the towers were there, the next they weren't. One day the lights went out and the floodwaters rose.

A clean beginning to our professional lives would be the day Russell interviewed me. *Long brown hair. Square ring.* But maybe our story begins further back, before I'm in it, when Russell was in his twenties, assuring a Catholic nun who'd been a spiritual advisor to two men on death row that he would not rest until the whole world had read her memoir. Nope, too far. Maybe it begins before *he's* in it. The night before I started at Vintage, I went to a party in Red Hook where the hosts had filled the bathtub with beer. Not bottles. Loose beer from a broken keg. They put a dog food cover over the drain as an extra seal. In the living room, I picked up a copy of *In Cold Blood* with the logo of my future employer on the spine. I was told to take the book home with me. But how did I get home? There were no cabs. I wouldn't have taken the subway at that time of night or decade.

Sometimes I think I am still there.

This is why New York stories make such sharp delineations. They're not trying to aggrandize the past, to lord it over the rest of the country; they're trying to pin it to the wall before it disintegrates. *See this? This was Disco.* In which case, it would behoove me to pick. Just pick a day when the lights went out and the floodwaters rose. So here it is:

On January 8, 2006, I walked into the office and did not take my coat off until noon. The phone, generally a one-way apparatus in a book publicist's office, was lighting up like a switchboard. On our monitors was an 18,000-word exposé, published on a website called *The Smoking Gun*, entitled "A Million Little Lies."

Technically, the trouble had begun a year prior, when Oprah selected *A Million Little Pieces* for her book club. It's author, James Frey, was her first contemporary choice after years of Faulkner and Tolstoy, and *The New York Times* had promised us a feature. This in itself was a coup for a book that had already been out in the world in hardcover. The day the news broke, I flung open my apartment door, pulled out the arts section, and marched to work, livid. No matter how many times I turned the pages, I couldn't make the story appear. I called Russell, fuming, but as I passed the stoops of my neighborhood, I saw: I couldn't find the story in the arts section because it was on the front page of *The New York Times*.

"Never mind," I said, and hung up.

Even we, whose jobs were to shoot for the moon and hit it, could not have anticipated this. The paper ran a photograph of Oprah and James onstage in Chicago. I am in the audience. I don't remember much from that trip apart from a makeup artist emerging during a commercial break to dab Oprah's leg with concealer. Afterward, we went to an Italian restaurant to celebrate. We were thrilled. Thrill is tough to remember.

As soon as I returned to New York, pressure started bearing down on us to get more press for the book. Sure, the thing is #1 on every list known to man, but how do we find new ways to jam it down America's throat? Under normal circumstances, this was the kind of challenge for which Russell lived. He was the most creative publicist I knew. His specialties were finding every crumb of attention left after a hardcover publication, or securing splashy coverage for books that had to have the dust blown off them. But the title in question was hardly plucked from obscurity. He talked back to the TV as Oprah explained how the book had found its way into her hands: "Could it be one of ten copies we FedExed? It's a mystery!"

The selection also coincided with a tsunami of media layoffs, not to mention the founding of Twitter. We watched in dread as our counterparts in journalism disappeared from their mastheads and then, with resignation, as the mastheads themselves disappeared. Every day, Russell found himself kicking the same sized balls into progressively narrowing goals, a taste of a future spent appeasing influencers who'd just as soon be reviewing scented candles. This one book became an internal bellwether: If we couldn't keep this juggernaut going, then what? We admired

Oprah's producers, whom we considered more capable than us by virtue of their access to power, but we were at the end of our rope. When we found ourselves on yet another conference call, discussing what further attention could be squeezed out of the universe without founding an entire news network, I broke:

"You guys, the *Today* show doesn't want your sloppy seconds."

As a rule, when one is on speaker, one should always be notified if Oprah is in the room.

"You're fired," Russell mouthed.

"*You're* fired," I mouthed back.

Finally, we hatched a plan so simple, so born of frustration, it was elegant: *A Million Little Pieces* was Oprah's first foray into living, breathing machismo, into "dude lit." *The New York Times* took us up on our offer for another interview. But by then, a counselor from the famed rehab facility Hazelden had begun questioning the veracity of the story. I warned James that he shouldn't antagonize the reporter. Amused by my concern, he called me afterward to tell me how proud I'd be: He'd asked the guy to turn the tape recorder off only twice.

I don't recall thinking well or poorly of James at that point. Only that it was a nice change of pace to be overseeing a publication with more sex appeal than a collection of newly translated Icelandic short stories (though, to each her own). I was young and, while not enamored of James, I was ambitious enough to feel the thrill of being a part of something *important*. Russell was different. Book editors are credited with being amateur therapists but a great book publicist will do the same for a dozen personalities at once, all the while bearing witness to what a book editor never sees: these people at their worst. After the art is done, all that's left is the ego. Russell thrived in this pond of bitter children and problematic geniuses. He gravitated toward underdogs. He would never put it in such sentimental terms, but he understood that real literature, like love, comes from a desire to be known.

There's not much point in me writing Russell a job recommendation at this juncture. But when I say he was a uniquely talented book publicist, I mean he could talk a publication that was considering mentioning a book into hosting a lecture series based on it. I mean that he saw the fiftieth anniversary of *Things Fall Apart* was approaching and a month later, he was escorting Chimamanda Ngozi Adichie, Edwidge Danticat, Toni Morrison, and Chinua Achebe himself across the stage at Town Hall. I mean you could stick a quarter in him, point to an obscure book, and out would pop a description so enticing, you'd want to skip work to read it. But it was more than that. His nerves ran through the hallways. When an author won an award, it was as if Russell could sense their whole childhoods, their unrequited crushes, their dysfunctional homes, the bullies that rode the school bus with this future titan of letters. Had Russell been there, he would have known. He would have recognized the extraordinary. The unspoken truth of our profession was that we wielded or sublimated our personalities in the name of people we held in our esteem. In return, the job protected us—protected him—from being ordinary. Even if he didn't *like* an author, he relished the chance to tangle with a worthy adversary. Russell's schema of "villain" came from *East of Eden*, from *Don Quixote*, from *All About Eve*.

But James was never this type of villain. He lacked the ingenuity. He reminded me of an Oscar Wilde quote one of my college classmates had tattooed on his forearm: "If I want to read something good, I'll write it."

Russell refused to accept bluster as a defense mechanism, not from some bro-ish figure who claimed artistic merit for white-knuckling his way through recovery. He'd spent his whole life on high alert for bro-ish figures. A kid from "nowhere by the sea," he'd landed at a rarified book publisher where he was delighted by the hierarchy. He was tickled by the hallowed temple of it all. He was obsessed, for instance, with where his staff went to school. If you graduated from Yale but did something idiotic, "It looks like they'll let anyone in these days." If you graduated from Shawnee State and did the same thing, "Well, it's no wonder." Or, apropos of nothing: "I need to stop hiring people from California." He didn't *actually* care about your background. Who was he to judge? What he was trying to tell you was that he remembered every last detail about you. You were worth getting to know because you, too, had taken shelter in the temple.

Alas, even when James tried not to bite the hand that fed him, he gnawed. He'd come from an industry where publicists are paid directly by their clients, and so he got in the habit of treating us like hired attack dogs ("I told them I'd have my publicist call"). "Good job" is not an inherently dirty phrase, but it translated as an attempt to establish power over people who would bear no immediate consequences from his success or failure. It's hard to put a number on it, but a publicist has to either make or annihilate five books in a row before she is promoted or fired. Mostly, Russell resented having to put all his energy into a single author, one who happened to be commandeering what little book coverage remained, one whose every presentation in the world ran in opposition to Russell's values. Ironically, he may have been the only person in book publishing who had no desire to make James go through his manuscript with a highlighter. He didn't need to hear confessions from a person he didn't trust.

There were, of course, other incidents and accidents along the road (much closer to the end of the road) that led to Russell's professional undoing, to his disillusionment with office life, to his perilous inability to maneuver through the future. If I want to identify anger so badly, all I have to do is imagine him over my shoulder, watching me devote this many words to James. But this is where the souring began. At least, this is the one where I was close enough to see every pore.

The night before we left for Christmas break, everyone had gone home except for Russell, who I could hear typing furiously down the hall. Not only was he stressed at work, he'd been on edge since the dramatic events of the summer. Something inside him had begun to shift. Legendary book editors were getting under his skin. Calls from agents, wondering why there wasn't more media for their clients, were becoming uncharacteristically terse. When an author accidentally deleted her tour schedule, Russell got so mad, he had to be talked into resending it. The idea that we were there to *protect* these people was slipping out the window. Too many of them were tedious pits of ingratitude.

On my desk was a manila envelope with James's medical records inside. We needed to see what the Minneapolis *Star Tribune* had seen. They were the ones who'd first floated the idea, publicly, that this guy might be more than just casually dishonest. The folder contained X-rays of the root canal James described in the book, for which he claimed to have received no anesthesia. I was looking at the pages when he called. See? Now everyone could see that he was telling the truth.

"Some people," I said, flicking the envelope's metal tab, "might say that no one is questioning if you had dental work done."

"What are they questioning?"

"There are no notes about you forgoing anesthesia."

"There probably aren't any notes about what I wore either."

Bolstered by a solid point, he decided it was his turn to ask the questions. He wanted to know if I'd ever done cocaine. I told him that I had, but if we were having a contest, I might not win. Well, then I could imagine how Novocain mimics the sensation of cocaine on the gums. I stared at my reflection in my office window, well-defined in the dark gap of the Hudson River. I'd had friends in recovery—for drugs, for alcohol, for eating too little, for having sex too much—but none who'd had holes drilled into their teeth at the same time. After we hung up, I googled "dental surgery" and "rehab," only to be met with tips on recovering from dental surgery.

I walked into Russell's office, chewing on my hair.

"I think we might have a problem."

"What did he do now?"

"I don't know."

"Well, whatever it is, he made his bed."

"Right. But I think there's a chance we might have to lie in it."

He stopped typing and wagged his finger at me.

"Let me tell you something: I am *not* going to an orgy with James Frey."

For all the narrative inconsistencies ("the lie of it," as Oprah would later call it, employing a tone more commonly reserved for serial killers) unearthed by *The Smoking Gun* (chief among them the fact that James had been in jail for two hours, not eighty-seven days) this bit about the relapse-triggering properties of Novocain never came up again. Which was a shame. Because I did want to know what was true and what wasn't. Because the thing about that Oscar Wilde quote is that it sure sounds good, but he never actually said it.

Eleven months before Russell died, I bumped into James in the lobby of a hotel in downtown Los Angeles. We were checking in at the same time and decided to grab a drink (soda for him). We were, after all, bonded by a unique experience.

When I published my first book, in 2008, I was told it needed a legal disclaimer, "you know, because of that whole James Frey thing." Yes, I knew it. Who but a handful of people could understand what had actually happened? Not our fellow book publicists, who gathered in their respective conference rooms with bowls of popcorn, waiting for James to get reamed out by Oprah. Not our other authors whose books were pushed into the shadows by a circus. Once, at a party, Russell and I were introduced to JT LeRoy's publicist. We were giddy at the prospect of *that* conversation but JT LeRoy was a hoax, not a scandal. A cardiac arrest patient and a brain tumor patient might share a similar psychological fallout but it's no use comparing notes after that.

All those years Russell and I spent wishing our authors would streak naked through a public park or commit a misdemeanor, *deflecting* attention was not in the orientation packet. At one point, I sought advice from a friend who was Kid Rock's publicist. This amounted to "no comment." Angry as Russell was with James for giving him the headache of the century, for putting him in the position of having to defend an author's character, no one could pin down the man's official crime. Hosing in the First Degree? But we knew this much: We'd never had to toss Martin Amis on *Larry King Live* to defend the "emotional truth" of his work.

James was relaxed and affable, sitting in the hotel bar, the world forever his beanbag. Like Russell, he took what he needed from the aura of old publishing and affirmed himself with it. Unlike Russell, he seemed able to tell himself that exile was an even *better* scenario. To be exiled is to be thought of twice. We could clutch the pearls right off our necks but he had broken the mold. As such, he'd always regarded me with a mix of friendliness and suspicion, both as a representative of an oppressive regime and as a cult member who'd almost but *not quite* been deprogrammed. We had a version of a friendship. One in which I allowed for the fact that he was both the subject of a witch hunt and a witch, and one in which he felt he'd been targeted by a moment whereas I felt he'd been granted clemency by it. If the scandal had happened now, he'd have been dragged over racial and class lines that went undisturbed at the time.

Before he walked onto Oprah's stage for that fateful second appearance, she'd warned him that she would be "rough" but there would be "redemption." This is not a secular word. It says a lot about how they each saw themselves. Regardless, redemption never came. Russell called me from backstage, apoplectic because "they tried to mic me up! As if I have anything to do with it!"

I heard the show before I saw it. A producer agreed to hold her phone up so I could listen live. Oprah read from my press release, confronting the book's publisher, Nan Talese: How could she have applied such effusive language when describing this pack of lies? Nan Talese is a one-woman publishing institution. Her authors include Margaret Atwood, Pat Conroy, and Ian McEwan. She has an eponymous imprint, a melodic mid-Atlantic accent, and a dizzying number of tasteful brooches. She is also one half of the most public literary marriage in modern history. If I'd waltzed into Nan Talese's office to get her approval on a press release, she would've gently escorted me out the door.

For us, the experience highlighted how little people knew or cared about book publishing, and we already suspected very little. Perhaps this seems like an inconsequential takeaway from the century's worst literary fiasco, but inconsequentiality was our manna. We had none of the perks of flashier industries, but suddenly we had all the culpability. What book publishing has, in exchange for units moved, is the presumption of good faith. There are no royalties split nineteen ways, no bananas duct-taped to the gallery wall. It's jarring to have that presumption replaced with a conspiracy theory. Worse, in order to explain the impossibility of a conspiracy, you have to cop to your own inefficacy. To being dragooned into someone else's morality play.

I remember not wanting to leave my office when the show was over. In three hours, twenty million viewers would see what I had just heard. I texted Russell.

How is he?

He's calling people, telling them he got, like, totally eviscerated.

How are you?

I hate everyone.

Afterward, Russell and I opened the letters. So many letters. We were still in range of the anthrax scares of the early aughts and a few of the envelopes contained white powder. Which turned out to be baby powder. But I can still see Russell, rushing past my office, pinching an envelope at arm's length. He got sent a bloody tooth, which he picked up with a tissue and dropped on my desk like a top, asking me if I thought it was real. *There are some questions in life, the very speaking of which are their own undoing.* I received a warped copy of the paperback, accompanied by a note explaining that the book in my hands had been pissed upon for as many days as James claimed he was in jail. The note was written on a pharmaceutical pad. I looked it up. It was for an antipsychotic medication.

James later told *The Guardian* that of the thousands of letters sent to him, only fifty had been hate mail. Which I'm sure is true.

What happens when you call someone a liar who, for whatever reason, might not believe he is lying? Shame has the reverse effect on such a person. One must be sure one sacrifices an actual virgin unless one wants a demon on one's hands. For weeks, James called the office to see if people were still talking about him. Who could blame him? Two-page spreads in *Us Weekly* had just been dedicated to his villainy. Russell maintained that none of it bothered him. God is a capitalist, tucking salvation into royalty checks.

In 2011, Oprah invited James on the show one final time, for one of her last episodes. The scandal had been a big deal, even by Oprah standards. She apologized for her lack of compassion five years prior. James, in the meantime, had commissioned a painting from the artist Ed Ruscha that read "PUBLIC STONING." Russell refused to watch the show, so I told him about the painting, about how Oprah had asked what it meant. James had said it was a reminder of this crucible of an experience but he was no victim. Russell snorted.

"She should've asked him what it was doing hanging in the living room."

Russell and I worked together for another five years, during which time the phones rang at a sporadic pace and the debacle faded into our rearview mirror. He still got plenty excited about the books, greeting us with facts he'd culled from them: *Did you guys know that Dolly the sheep is named after Dolly Parton? Did you guys know that kids these days have better thumb dexterity than we do?* He still laughed until he looked like someone had stuck a bow tie on a balloon. But he was spikier now that he'd seen how easily blame could be laid at his feet and how, if another James came along, commanding his attention, it would be his job to give it. All those years spent banging the drum for the underappreciated and the underpulsed was never his real job. His real job was to keep the agents quiet, the editors looking good, and the authors from sticking their fingers in the light sockets.

It wasn't long before Russell's formerly targeted discernment morphed into widespread exasperation, his quips grafted from some other arena of his life. For years, he'd seemed so removed from the harsh realities of book publishing, but now his story was becoming the story of his environment: stymied, scared, self-censuring, scrambling for relevance. The reason I hadn't noticed that pieces of our world had been falling from the ceiling was because Russell had sheltered me from the debris. And by the time I did notice, our world was already gone.

I was already gone.

In the months after I quit, I was terribly homesick. Working from home felt lawless. And quiet. I had difficulty getting anything done without Russell hovering over me, wanting to play. I also felt adrift in a literary landscape outside the office walls, one that liked to signal intelligence with obscurity. I'd taken for granted the calm that came with being in the orbit of legendary writers. I'd spent my last day at Vintage escorting Alice Munro around town and, during a lull in the conversation, I asked her if people ever recognized her on the street. She thought for a moment and said: "On my better days, I think they do. On my worse days, I think they're thinking, 'What a sweet little old lady, I hope she doesn't die in front of me.'"

Russell practically changed the locks on the building. He took every opportunity to make sure I knew I was not welcome back, not through the service entrance anyway. Why would I care about office gossip? Why would I want to come to Midtown for lunch? Did I seriously buy myself the same desk chair I'd had at work? *Shoo, shoo.*

In a funny way, he reminded me of my grandmother. Aside from the projectile pearl bracelet, the other gift she gave me (while she was alive) was an onyx bracelet. This was after my mother informed her I'd become the editor of my high school literary magazine. A loop of black beads arrived in the mail. No note. It's no coincidence that both these items were presented on occasions of academic achievement. It's also probably no coincidence that they are black and white, symbolic encouragement to free myself from the gray area, to escape the middle, to protect myself from the ordinary. To go be *special*. But that was their priority, hers and Russell's. Their deathly fear of the reverse.

What I never told Russell was that in the same way his specialness had found an annex in great authors or inanimate objects, mine had found an annex in him. For those precious weeks when he was still around but the jewelry was gone, I wanted it back because it was mine. But once they were both gone? I wanted it back because it was him. Because I could no longer picture it without picturing the times he held it, without associating it with his approval. I had stored everything I liked best about myself in Russell. Now he would hardly let me access it. A preview of what it might feel like if he ever up and decided to burn the whole book.

ACT 3: THE DESCENT

Anger is a cousin of intelligence. If you are not revolted by certain things, you have no boundaries. If you have no boundaries, you have no self-knowledge. If you have no self-knowledge, you have no taste, and if you have no taste, why are you here? Russell taught me that. He taught me to be selective about who I jumped for and how high. This is a vital skill in a profession where accomplishment can start to look a lot like subservience. You find yourself writing even-tempered responses to e-mails from unhappy authors, cc'ing ten of your colleagues about how brainless you are. You learn to navigate your job in a way that those in your sister vocations never have to navigate theirs. A film assistant can eliminate a name from a guest list without gambling with the fate of the film. What recourse is there for a book publicist except to answer e-mails at a slightly slower pace?

Once, near the end of my time at Vintage, an author canceled his tour on account of a broken foot. He assured me he'd do anything else I asked. But when the writing assignments rolled in, requests for a list of favorite films or a description of a memorable meal, he demurred. He demurred in all caps: TELL THEM I BROKE MY GODDAMN FOOT.

I typed: *Your writing foot?*

But Russell's brittleness was starting to rub off on the assistants, too. They had not been on the job long enough to wield a bad attitude, to roll their eyes at straightforward requests from journalists. They were too young to lose patience, but thanks to Russell? They never had any. And as for the authors? Well. No matter how abject their genius, there was only one of them. One life in one university town, needing this one book to do well. An economy-destroying meteor had hit their careers yet their children's tuition fees remained just as due, their boilers just as broken. Russell seemed frightened of their thinly veiled desperation. As if, by behaving in a pathetic fashion, they might make him pathetic too. They might shatter whatever illusions remained.

I could hear him coming. He'd clomp down the hall and pace in front of my desk before yelling *through* me about an e-mail I'd forwarded to him. The kind of e-mail that would not warrant a mention, much less a conversation, in the old days. Outbursts once reserved for high-profile problems were now directed toward, say, a nonprofit organization in Dallas wanting copies of Colson Whitehead's latest novel for their gala gift bags. All the other publishing houses had agreed to donate. We wouldn't want our author to be embarrassed, would we?

"You tell them absolutely, we would. These books aren't going to charity. They're going to people who can afford to buy them! They want us to be complicit in robbing an author of royalties. These socialites, they think everything is owed to them. If they want to talk about a bulk order, they can call me. Until then— who's asking again?"

"A children's hospital."

"They can go fuck themselves. Can we do Chinese for lunch or are you sick of it?"

The first complaint was filed forty-eight hours after I left the company. An allegation of "sexual harassment, basically," leveled against a gay man by a straight woman, may not be the most frequently ordered dish on the menu but all the ingredients are there.

"That's a neat trick," I said, when Russell finally told me.

He did not want to tell me. I bullied it out of him by threatening to come up to the house. An etiquette obsessive ("You're not bringing *flowers* to a dinner party, are you?"), he was embarrassed to be charged with not operating well in the world. To make matters worse, his behavior was so consistently bad, it needed to be articulated to the authorities. But by whom, I wondered? Was this not the same man who unloaded boxes of chocolates from grateful authors, wordlessly reaching over cubicle walls and shaking them in their paper cups? Was it not the same man who brought in cartons of fresh eggs every Monday? On the one hand, I couldn't isolate a suspect. On the other, "literally anyone" seemed like a solid guess.

There was that time he decided an editor was "dressed like a flight attendant on Provincetown Airlines." Or that time my assistant showed up to work wearing a cardigan with a row of over-worked buttons and Russell exclaimed: "It's like you marched into Talbots and said, 'Give me the sluttiest thing you have!'" Or the hundred times he asked me if I "got dressed in the dark."

I never saw the complaint, but it was submitted by a freshly minted college graduate with a conviction that she was overdue for a promotion the moment the flash went off for her photo ID. We overlapped for about six months before I quit. I was on vacation when Russell had his head turned by her Ivy League credentials. Her voice was soft and ingratiating, likely forged by years of leaving voice mails for professors, requesting extensions. I used to feign a lot of closed-door emergencies. She must've thought my life was in shambles. The idea that Russell was lording *sex* over this person would require a shift in personality more than a shift in sexual orientation. When she started messing up, he sat her down, told her what could be improved. Spell-checking a press release, for example. When she failed to supercharge her work ethic, he didn't have the heart to fire her. Instead, he ignored her. And it could get quite chilly outside the perimeter of Russell's light.

"But surely," I said, "there's a difference between an unhappy workplace and a hostile one."

"Oh, there is. That's why the complaint isn't really about her. It's about you."

"Come again?"

He cleared his throat and began reading. Here, in paragraph 4, subsection C, you will note my full name, former job title, and the date on which Russell referred to me as a "toothless hooker" because I declined to get coffee with him.

"I mean, you did say that."

Over the coming years, Russell would face several complaints of this genre. We never got into details for nebulous legal reasons but also because there was nothing to discuss. We'd met. *You could do a whole spin-off about that one.* His mascot days were over. The corporate spotlight had turned into a heat lamp. He was being watched—targeted, rather—for inappropriate behavior, for anything that would end in a lawyer and a check. There was an assistant on another floor with whom he neglected to share movie screeners, freebies he distributed for fun. She complained that Russell was "mean" to her. He was forced to take her out to lunch. That way she wouldn't think he was mean anymore.

By the time he died, Russell seemed on board with keeping employees away from the house. Living in isolation was preferable to living in fear. What if he said something offensive while refilling someone's wineglass? "We're hibernating this summer," he'd say, putting a jovial spin on it. He was petrified. But he was also pissed. It's hard to say which state is more detrimental to being a professional cheerleader, but it's angering to craft a life in which you can tolerate participating, only to have it attract people who want to dismantle it, to be told that the same personality that built this place is now a liability.

I'd been so busy missing the world I left, I had not stopped to think of how I'd left him in it. After he died, I attempted to pump my former coworkers for more information. How had things gotten so bad? One of them texted me: *He was so loved but also a wild animal in a cage at work. It was too much to bottle up and keep in an office.*

Fair enough. I'd witnessed the blurring of lines, the frustrations with work, the poisonous boredom. Idle hands with sharp nails.

Even overseeing the once-in-a-lifetime media explosion that was *Fifty Shades of Grey* was not enough to keep Russell feeling settled and, arguably, made things worse—the last thing this man needed was a box of promotional handcuffs under his desk. Book publicity had become about colonizing other planets now that ours was dying, and Russell tried to adapt. He oversaw movie-tie-in editions, planned social media stunts, and attended Comic-Con (developing a newfound respect for cosplay). He became close with E. L. James as they traveled the country together, doing signings in hotel ballrooms, taking selfies beneath billboards. He seemed to have a fluency in what she was selling. And she'd come along at a time when Russell was desperate for a sliver of his former glory. Was this the same person who'd once turned up his nose at Dan Brown, who used to joke that if aliens needed a core sample of humanity, we should show them to the Vintage book room? Who cared when her books were spawning paper shortages? Plus, he understood E. L. James. She'd started out as an outsider, as well. An underdog. Which, along with the Edies of the world, was his favorite type of person.

Still, I shudder to think of Russell in a marketing meeting, having flown in from a sex toy conference the night before. He once told me he'd threatened to whip an editorial assistant with a promotional toy but "not really."

"Not really you didn't say it or not really you didn't mean it?"

"The second."

Russell's teasing had lost its sugar coating at the exact wrong moment in history, when little infractions got swallowed down the same pipe as big ones, when his boundless energy read as aggression. And yet, the consequences were unforeseeable to him. He was, in fact, confounded. He'd spent his whole life playing for Team Oversensitive and overnight he'd been traded to Team Callous. He knew from misogynists and megalomaniacs. He had no interest in taking credit for anyone else's success. He used his spare time to fight for their raises. But none of that mattered anymore.

I suppose what Russell never understood is that if you are a recent college graduate living in the twenty-first century, the name of the game is not to play the game. The learning curve for the establishment has proven too steep and your peers have been sought out to translate the contemporary world, to turn on the Wi-Fi. They're not gunning for a seat at the table. They're gunning for the table. The catch with book publishing is that, despite manufacturing the product with the richest history of inciting incendiary behavior, it remains deeply antiquated. This is not because senior staffers had to put up with being snubbed in the hallway so why shouldn't you? It's because the entire machinery is driven by the one art form that takes longest to produce, release, consume, and profit from. Any industry that sees itself as *that* scrappy is going to be painfully slow to wrap itself around the idea that it has the capacity to hurt its own.

What must all this be like for a criminally underpaid assistant? It must feel like being hazed by invalids. Then, just when you're about to go blind from personalizing press releases, Russell pops up like a prairie dog over your cubicle wall, asking why you're wearing the same outfit two days in a row.

Perhaps the younger generations would say I'm revealing the number of rings on my trunk here. I should know better. It is not they who need protecting but all of us, as a society based on a foundation of mutual respect, fairness, and sensitivity. I have felt how much easier it would be to align myself with their side of the generational courtroom. For one thing, I find myself at an age where one wants to appear younger but must make certain conversational sacrifices to do so, a transitional period between taking credit for one's experience and swallowing that experience, lest one reveal one was around to witness the Pleistocene. For another, it's difficult to champion nuance when most people in positions of power abuse the definition.

My generation (X, Millennial Rising) invented depression but is seriously lacking in revolution. We are the last group of Americans to be socially conscious while not doing anything about it. Us, with our vague awareness of Earth Day and biannual outrage over systemic racism and sorrow about distant earthquakes from which we never shook. We were not promised the world, no, but at least we grew up with a semblance of an economy. At least we had a path. Then we let the wind take the breadcrumbs out of disaffection. So if you are younger, you might ask: How many future generations must we punish with our inherited bad habits? We don't even have good thumb dexterity, for fuck's sake. If you are younger, you might say: Sorry about that episode with the ozone layer that you half-wits thought was gonna be *the* thing but open your eyes. We don't have time for this.

Saving the planet and eradicating inequality is a tall order for an English lit major. But maybe she can start in her own back-yard. Maybe she can start by not tolerating little *comments* from some out-of-touch madman in a bow tie. You tell me: What makes him any different than the rest?

Any industry that makes a habit of toasting forty-year anniversa-ries is bound to incur some serious mortalities. But after Russell died, they were bizarrely concentrated. His death, which already felt marginalized to me, was like a pool-ball break for more deaths. In the months following Russell's suicide, giants of the publishing world disappeared. The beloved Random House edi-tor Susan Kamil died. Sonny Mehta, the legendary editor in chief of Knopf, died. Carolyn Reidy, the longtime head of Simon & Schuster, died. A generation of mentors, wiped off the map. How strange it must have been for the assistants during this time period, going home to their roommates and explaining that their bosses kept keeling over.

The string of losses reminded me of Donald Barthelme's mor-dant short story "The School," about a grade school teacher tasked with explaining a series of increasingly significant deaths:

One day, we had a discussion in class. They asked me, where did they go? The trees, the salamander, the tropical fish, Edgar, the poppas and mommas, Matthew and Tony, where did they go? And I said, I don't know, I don't know. And they said, who knows? And I said, nobody knows. And they said, is death that which gives meaning to life? And I said, no, life is that which gives meaning to life.

142 | SLOANE CROSLEY

I played it on a loop: Russell and Susan and Sonny, where did they go? I don't know, I don't know. Nobody knows.

The last time I saw Sonny was at Russell's memorial service in October 2019. He died a couple of months later, on December 30, 2019. It was glaring how unable I was to mourn Sonny. This man was not some coda for Russell's story. His death was a global heartbreak. He also happened to have been personally responsible for the drunkest I'd ever been at the office, having once taken me for an actual three-martini lunch. It was Sonny who stepped over Russell and me that day, when I tackled Russell to the floor. It was his voice above us: *Children.* But I was too jealous to be sad. Every word about his life, about all their remarkable lives, was a stab in the eye.

Russell never got an obituary. He was not an editor and he was not famous. Book publicity: thankless until the last stop. Russell's partner was too overwhelmed with grief to contact newspapers, and by the time the rest of us campaigned for an obituary, arguing for Russell's importance, it was too late. The window had closed. Or maybe we didn't try hard enough. A half dozen current and former publicists and *this* was the story we couldn't place? But we were beaten by the nature of the beast. Suicide, itself such an isolating death, wants its mourning to be solitary. It wants you to scatter and shrink, for everyone to curl up in their respective balls. We had a hard time fighting it. By the time all those editors passed away ("died," Russell would correct me, "classy people say 'died'"), I felt he was robbed. And I did not react well.

Is there such a thing as a funeralzilla? When my former colleagues secured a space for a memorial service, I did my best to make them regret consulting me. I objected to everything. I wanted something small. Dinner at an expensive restaurant. And we were to serve only Russell's favorite foods. No fucking dill. And only certain people should give speeches and they shouldn't drone on. No one had the heart to say: "You do realize he will not be *attending* the dinner?" Fine, then. If we must do something bigger, it should be massive. And the programs should be fastened with ribbon, not staples. Actually, maybe we shouldn't do it at all. All those people, stuck in their chairs like they're getting a lecture on the Constitution. Maybe we should do it outside. Is it hard to shut down Fifth Avenue for an hour?

It took a small army to get it through my skull that people needed to mourn, and not just Russell's five favorite people. A few more than that. They needed to sit in an auditorium and listen to speeches and poems, and some of those poems might be Auden. This is not actually about Russell. More to the point, it's not about me. I am not the sole protector of this man. If he were here, he could manage the guest list, but he's not here. The needs of the living are more important than the wants of the dead. Can't I understand? Not as important. More important.

In the end, the only decision I made was to wear a dress I liked but Russell hated, and shoes Russell liked but I hated. This seemed like a fair compromise, considering. I wrote a eulogy. So did others. Our stories had so much duplicate fiber. But other people seemed to have no problem accessing their anger at Russell. Their heartbreak wires (*I miss him*) were entangled with their rage wires (*I'll kill him*). They were in pain too, of course. If a rising tide lifts all boats, a whirlpool pulls them all to the bottom.

The same way I had to pass the restaurant where I last saw him just to leave the house, they had to pass his empty office just to get to the bathroom.

Backstage, I saw his partner, who did not speak, who could not speak. We hugged. I hadn't seen him since the parking lot in Connecticut, and before that? Not for years. He smelled like the fireplace and garlic. Russell's garlic. John Updike wrote, "Every marriage tends to consist of an aristocrat and a peasant." I'm sure their roles were perfectly obvious from the inside, but I never knew who was who when we were eating cobbler straight from the pan. Or when Russell dove into the pool while the dogs paced the perimeter, barking with concern.

Once, when I was still working in the office, a former co-worker created "Vintage Books Mad Libs" and sent them to us:

Then I ran into Sloane in the hall. I asked: "How is Russell?"
"Oh, he's _____. But he thinks he's getting
      (ADJECTIVE)

_____."
  (ADJECTIVE)

"His poor partner."
"His poor partner," Sloane agreed. "It's a shame. He's so

_____."
  (ADJECTIVE)

"And Russell can be such a _____."
         (NOUN)

I will never know what his partner dealt with or how hard he tried. I will never know exactly what happened up at that house, either for the years I spent in the yellow room or the years I spent outside it. And it is not mine to know. That's someone else's love story.

"I'm so sorry," I whispered, my chin on his shoulder.

He pulled away and looked down.

"Sweetie," he said, resting his palm on my cheek, "what wonderful shoes."

This is how the world ends, right, not with a bang but a whimper? After the service, I would not have minded a bang. Perhaps I could have slapped someone during the cocktail hour. Or run into the street, screaming. Perhaps a single scream on a bridge at sunset, mouth agape. In Norwegian, the title of Munch's masterpiece also translates to "The Shriek." Maybe the words have the same meaning in Norwegian, but there's quite a difference in English. A shriek is more involuntary. It's pain going in, not pain going out. It's seeing a mouse in the kitchen. When it comes to Russell, I have no further interest in shrieking.

But the anger is either not forthcoming or is so waylaid, I won't know it's about him when it arrives. Russell taught me well. Outrage and indignation have an intellectual feel, but anger is guttural. Some element of the world did not hold up its end of the bargain and anger is the debt collector. I would like to get good and furious with *someone*. Perhaps with his partner, with myself, with Russell, with our lopsided fiefdom that demanded everything—loyalty, persistence, humility—and gave us only each other in return. Then it took that away too. We did everything right, didn't we? We closed our eyes and opened our arms and walked through the temple door. They say everyone is selling something. All Russell ever wanted was to sell the world on itself, one good story at a time.

I did try screaming once, just to see how it felt.

This was on the one-year anniversary of his death: July 27, 2020. A curious thing about the anniversary of a suicide is the increased likelihood for premeditation. This is not just the day that a person you loved died, it's the day they knew they would die. You wake up in the morning and think: Maybe he didn't know yesterday or the day before, but he probably knew today. He probably knew tonight. It's a strange comfort. With each passing moment, I found myself feeling closer to Russell than I had all year. We watched the sun rise. We ate dumplings. We read James Baldwin's *Go Tell It on the Mountain*. Then we strolled along the Hudson River, down Pier 34, a concrete strip with no pretense of being a destination. It's just there and back.

New York had thinned out by then. The plague had settled in, pushing out the outside world. People were inside their apartments or had fled for other area codes, the city's warm weather showing off for an absentee audience. I looked down the river, to the Statue of Liberty, so lonely these days, and I turned to Russell and asked: *Would you have survived this? With everything that was already so wrong, would you have survived what came next?*

Then I lowered my face mask to scream but no sound came out.

PART IV

DO THE MONKEYS

MISS US?

(DEPRESSION)

The ceiling had been coming down for years. Water and to-bacco had stained it from both sides. Comets appeared where there were no comets, trailing streaks of asbestos. But if you looked carefully, you'd notice—will still notice—a bigger prob-lem with the ceiling in Grand Central. The entire sky is applied backward. West is east and east is west. A commuter spotted the mistake in 1913, shortly after the building opened to the public. At the time, the party line from the city was that the ceiling was meant to mimic what God sees when he looks down, not what humans see when they look up. But no matter. Then, in 1997, it was refurbished to its original cerulean color, the dirt sponged off, the constellations lit up, and it was so beautiful, no one cared if they were looking up at God or if God was looking down at them.

Or if God wasn't looking at all.

It's a thirty-minute train ride from the city of White Plains, where I grew up, into Grand Central Terminal. Which means I must have been inside the building plenty of times before the renovations. But I can't produce a single memory of it. Just when I think I can, I realize I'm watching Cary Grant on the run in *North by Northwest* or Robin Williams making the crowd waltz in *The Fisher King*. Grand Central is how those of us who grew up in the northern suburbs were born into the city, and much like birth, I have no recollection of it. I remember the city itself. The graffiti. The potholes. The smell of marzipan wafting out of bakeries. The fifty-cent tour of my father's childhood in Brighton Beach: *We used to pull seahorses out of this water!* A homeless man in Rockefeller Center, screaming about how Kitty Dukakis was an alcoholic because she drank rubbing alcohol. For a long time, I thought you weren't an alcoholic *unless* you drank rubbing alcohol.

Grand Central comes into focus only in my twenties. Age 21: Sprinting from the Hammerstein Ballroom to make the last train home, flinging my body in the direction of the correct track. Age 22: Losing my ticket in the dressing room of Canal Jeans and having to pay for a more expensive one on the train (this is a tragedy where I come from, the behavior of a garbage person). Age 23: Blushing when a bartender compliments my dress in a way that makes me fold my coat over it the whole way home, like a human burrito.

At the information booth inside the main concourse, you can still find one of the more unheralded constants of New York life: the paper train schedules. White Plains is on the blue line, the Harlem Line. It's a straight shot to the priciest hamlets in America but I always thought of it as an everyman's blue, a municipal blue, the kind of blue you see on a library card. As far as I was concerned, the green line, the Hudson Line, dropped passengers off directly at bed-and-breakfasts. It was for people who wanted to dangle off the grid. As for the red line, the New Haven Line? I would've felt more comfortable running away to Rio. Did they have cabs in suburban Connecticut? Buses? Signage? Eye contact? This was the red of mutual funds, of apples injected with poison.

And yet all of these people, rich and poor, talented and talentless, entered New York the same way I did. Maybe they'd always dreamed of living here. Or maybe this choice, which can be so difficult for outsiders, was the easiest. Then we scattered like marbles, coded with the understanding that we had no real story, that unlike people from faraway places, who parlayed their roots into something profound, we'd have to brush over our blank spaces indefinitely. But there *is* a language to the suburbs. None of us came from places known for their grit or their splendor, so this language is easily muffled. We muffle it ourselves when we grab on to the city's coattails as if we're borrowing something. We are not borrowing anything. We are like the horses in Central Park in that our story is defined by what we're looking at.

So who owns this town? Who feels for it the most when it hurts? When tragedy strikes, a tacit competition plays itself out until the number of blocks you were away from that exploding manhole cover gets fewer with each telling. If the city ever dies and goes to heaven, perhaps it will be revealed that it was us all along, us half-natives/half-tourists who have felt both held and snubbed by New York, who know the default and the desire, who see it the most clearly. But not likely.

September 2001: The downtown 9 train. A disturbance on the tracks. The subway rattled, moved backward, something I have never experienced before or since, and released us into Times Square. I knew a girl from college who worked as a temp in the World Trade Center. She woke up that morning and decided to blow off work and sit in Central Park with a Discman, emerging around noon. I sometimes think of those bonus hours of innocence she smuggled with her, into the new world. August 2003: A city unplugged. Computer monitors dark, we walked down flights of stairs until our knees hurt. That night, my neighbor, whose husband had been on the 104th floor of the North Tower, hosted a dinner-by-flashlight. For some reason, her dead husband's parents had granted a Canadian documentary crew permission to interview her about her loss. She opened the window and yelled at them to fuck off until they left. Then she lit a joint off a candle and said: "I hope they get stuck in the Lincoln Tunnel." October 2012: Windows taped, air-conditioning unit whistling, boyfriend in California. I might hang up on you, I said. Nothing personal. Suddenly, a horrific sound. The building around the corner was not up to code and the entire façade collapsed into a pile of rubble. Which turns out to be a fantastically noisy thing, a façade collapsing. My boyfriend suggested I get out of there. I felt around for a corkscrew.

"But where on earth would I go?"

March 2020: As if with a snap of the fingers, the quiet. In the future, it will be up to clever middle school teachers to slip this into the curriculum. We grew up with a version of it: *The first*

thing you'd notice about eighteenth-century New York is the smell.
The first thing you'd notice about pandemic New York was the
standstill that has been described by a thousand writers and will
be described by a thousand more and none of us will nail it. If we
even want to anymore. We barely noticed the noise when it returned. Noise is sanity. All that quiet, peppered by the wailing of
ambulances. On 9/11, nurses lined up outside St. Vincent's, poking their heads down Seventh Avenue, waiting for wounded that
never came. But they did come. They were just late.

We let go of so much so quickly. Really lost the plot. Within
weeks, New York, which epitomizes such an embarrassment of
freedoms in the global imagination, had become a white-collar
prison. Was there anything so wrong in any given moment? No.
Was everything an unmitigated disaster? Yes. We went shopping
for tuna, liquor, garlic, scallions, lentils, bagels to freeze, greens
to blanch, wedges of parmesan. Eucalyptus tea. Helps with lung
function. Zinc lozenges. Stops the throat from turning into a
petri dish. Oximeters. Let's hope not. Crank radios. Because
zombies. Some people carted home toilet paper in cumulous
bulk. Dress for the disease you want, I suppose. Apparently, what
a lot of people wanted was cholera.

It was assumed that freelancers such as myself would be
uniquely suited to the impending trials of quarantine because
we already worked from home, cordoned off from polite society.
*The author lives in Manhattan, where she divides her time between
her kitchen and her living room.* True, we were no strangers to
self-structure. But this meant we knew exactly how much uncer-
tainty we could sustain and we were already at maximum capacity. We were, every last one of us, injected into the last paragraph

of James Joyce's "The Dead." The grief, for ourselves, for one another, for our city, was like snow, "falling on every part of the dark central plain, on the treeless hills, falling softly upon the Bog of Allen and, farther westward, softly falling into the dark mutinous Shannon waves. It was falling, too, upon every part of the lonely churchyard on the hill where Michael Furey lay buried."

Russell was my Michael Furey.

Here is one dead person. Now here come the rest.

For twelve days in March, I lay in bed and watched the sky brighten, the gentle but inevitable tap of a new day. This kind of insomnia was familiar to me. Those living with grief know the particular sleeplessness it engenders—so nonnegotiable, so immune to warm milk and narcotics. Typical insomnia has an apologetic feel, like it doesn't want to be here any more than you do. Like it knows you have a big day tomorrow but it can't help itself. Grief insomnia has a mouth on it: *Time does not heal all wounds. Time does not heal any wounds. Who promised you that? Get your money back.* Time only pushes wounds aside. Regular life becomes insistent and crowds out the loss. Usually, this is a good thing. So much of healing is the recognition that not all your tissue got damaged in the accident. But every so often, there is no such thing as regular life. Every so often, life crowds out loss with more loss.

Our collective thirst for horrors was insatiable, which didn't make us feel like catastrophists; it made us feel like taking attendance. What about the cabdrivers? What about the umbrella guys who manifest at the first drop? What about the theater?

There's no such thing as a one-woman audience. What about the zoos? Do the monkeys miss us? Animals sense these things, you know. My brain was like a spooky little child who wouldn't stop showing me disturbing drawings. *You know what would make this even easier? If you looked at your phone. You know you want to.* As the writer and theologian Thomas Merton wrote, "The more you try to avoid suffering, the more you suffer, because smaller and more insignificant things begin to torture you, in proportion to your fear of being hurt. The one who does most to avoid suffering is, in the end, the one who suffers most." So I looked at my phone.

In theory, I should've been equipped to deal with the phantasmagoria of the missing. Missing objects. Missing people. Missing worlds. It all goes. Sometimes it gets ripped away. But the catch, at least at the very beginning, was that nothing was actually gone. Not yet. One imagines reporting a stolen city: *Ma'am, let us know when something turns up missing.*

I'd spent no small amount of time, in the months after Russell died, daydreaming about how *luxurious* it would be to prepare for loss. Turns out the prepared version is not so hot. Perhaps this is the plainest definition of anxiety: mourning what isn't gone yet. Anxiety is an ever-present stage of grief, a shadow attached to the heels of its more infamous siblings. If you look closely, you'll see it in the background of all the family photographs. But how else is one meant to handle an invisible threat? American children of the 1980s were introduced to this existential dilemma in *The Never-Ending Story*, a film that features a malevolent force called the Nothing. The Nothing rolls in like a storm and destroys the world of Fantasia by absorbing all its stories. In the same way, a cloud of medical-grade anxiety had descended upon the city, creating a depressive mind-meld. This is an unnatural state for New York to find itself in. I should never know what anyone is thinking.

It's a strange thing, to have someone you love, someone with a lot of opinions, die before a global catastrophe. Nora Ephron died three years before Donald Trump announced his candidacy, and I still think about this. One is relieved for the dead, that they were spared the news, but frustrated to be robbed of their reaction. One fantasizes about being the messenger: *You're never gonna believe it.* I could not know what Russell would make of this time or what we'd talk about. Or how often. Being confined to the house in Connecticut, where he hadn't spent more than two consecutive weeks in twenty years, would be a challenge. He also tended to mirror his partner and retreat under stress. He was, for a professional publicist, not a big phone person.

I could, however, ask an age-old question: What would Russell do? The flea market would be on indefinite hiatus. On weekends, he would grab a bucket of fish food and wade into the pond, far from the cocked heads of the dogs. Then he'd watch the bright bodies of the fish snap back and forth as he showered them with pellets. At night, he would probably watch old movies or *Judge Judy*, and in the morning, he'd read by the pool. He would be there still when his partner returned from the supermarket.

"I swear," his partner might say, "no one knows how to behave."

"Have they ever?" Russell might reply, not looking up from his book.

And he would take pictures. *Loads* of pictures. Russell was constantly posting photos of his garden, so I did as he would have done, sharing images of the trees in Washington Square Park, their branches heavy with cherry blossoms. Or the tulips yawning open on my block (the spring made a mockery of us all—we could smell the lilacs through our masks). When an acquaintance in Chicago scolded me to "get back inside!" I typed, "That's my time in the yard, bitch," but deleted it. A week later, when I shared a video of the Mister Softee man outside Tompkins Square Park, dropping sprinkles onto my cone, she wrote, "Shouldn't he pull his mask up?"

Was it worth it, hearing from people not in New York? Prior to Covid, this question was the purview of local lunatics who think this place is the still point of the turning world. And even they didn't ask it seriously. Now it was given real consideration. If my recent spate of losses had taught me anything, it was that just because other people have experienced the same trauma, that doesn't mean you have to talk to them about it. What photographic record of city life might this woman have preferred? There was a delivery truck parked on my block that used to be a Walmart truck. At night, under the streetlamps, you could see the reflection of where the logo had once been. It was full of dead bodies. How much tragedy were we meant to provide those who needed us to be falling apart to the tune of one calamitous note?

We were not depressed all the time, no. Sometimes we were drunk. Sometimes we let joy tumble into our nets. I passed between two advertisements, positioned across the street from each other. For a banking app: "Made for staying put." For a toothpaste: "Spread it around." I bummed a cigarette off a friend from seven floors up. He wrapped a lighter and a cigarette in a tinfoil pouch and threw it out the window like a set of keys. For another friend's birthday, also a smoker, I bought her brand of cigarettes, removed one from the fresh pack, and replaced it with a candle. During a walk, I lit the candle, holding it between us, an oddly romantic gesture. She lowered her mask, made a wish, and blew directly into my face.

See? Funny.

Even if I'd wanted to, it's hard to take a picture of one's fear of dying alone or dying in general. Hard to put a filter on an open-ended dystopia. Harder still to take a picture of the realization that one's best friend is truly gone, a stage of grief that arrived at a pretty inconvenient time.

At night, the hole in my heart was like a wind tunnel that whistled straight through until dawn. As the hours grew darker, I laughed at my ceiling, replaying pops and flashes of Russell, the memory of him and the memory of New York intertwining: The time we saw Anthony Weiner on the subway and Russell marched off the train in protest, got his bag caught in the door, and Anthony Weiner pushed it out. The time a cashier at Ricky's asked if he was my dad. My going-away drinks at the Russian Samovar, when Russell claimed the horseradish vodka was making him cry. The time we crashed a party at the Indian consulate and Russell accidentally locked himself in the bathroom. My fortieth birthday dinner, when he ate magic mushrooms for the first time, wrapped himself in a friend's tablecloth, and walked out with it. The time we walked into an awards dinner and I instructed him to get me out of a specific conversation, should such a conversation happen. When it did happen, Russell marched across the room and said: "I'm sorry to interrupt, I was going to come over here and make up some ridiculous story about why I needed her, but she has to wake up early for an elective surgery and it's nothing to be ashamed of, even at her age—should you be drinking?"

Then I'd run out of my nightly stipend of memories and lie there in silence, wishing I could graft some of that silence onto those evenings when Russell and I walked home along the park, competing for airtime. What words would have flooded in if we'd let them?

In *The Year of Magical Thinking*, Didion writes: "A single person is missing for you, and the whole world is empty."

Also true: The whole world is empty, and a single person is missing for you.

I no longer felt Russell's presence, no longer sat on the stoop and spoke to him. The restaurant was closed now, the windows covered from the inside with newspaper. But I sensed he'd left town. The membrane had hardened so that even if I knew where to press, it wouldn't matter anymore. When it came to creating my own stories, I'd been playing for an audience of one for so long. Russell was my litmus test. Would this amuse him? Would he find it silly? I'd never published a word when he wasn't alive, when I didn't know him. Quarantine was doing its best to wipe all our short-term memories (prove to me it's Wednesday), but without Russell as my witness, I could feel it setting its sights on my long-term memory too. What *was* my story? I scavenged for facts and frowned at the haul: Woman. Jewish. Allergic to pecans. An assembly of details. Is this what makes a person?

Shortly before the pandemic, a former coworker had sent me an envelope she'd found in Russell's desk. It was full of letters I'd written to him over the years on hotel stationery, some fancy, some from pads hardly worth the glue. I used to drop the letters off at various front desks, at ungodly hours, while on book tour. They had such life in them. They were written from a person who felt more definite, to a person who was, in the literal sense, more definite. They featured elaborate sketches of Marriott parking lots or read, simply, "Is *that* what you're wearing today?" Now the letters lived in my desk drawer, in the apartment I never left.

I was losing him and yet I couldn't get away from him.

As the pandemic settled in, we made an effort not to compete for Most Aggrieved in Group. Ego, as it turns out, is depression's comorbidity. We aimed for solemnity, tried not to let our individual stories bounce off the force fields of other stories. Was this not the imposed collective trial for which the MTA had been training us our entire lives? We are New York strong. We are New York tough.

But who, I wonder, is weak? Pittsburgh?

We kept our bodies moving, feeling baptized by the wind as we walked across barren bridges, speculating about the inside of hotels, all those entombed carts of free toiletries. Russell had a long-running frugality scheme, seeing how long he could last without paying for shampoo. The bathroom in Connecticut featured bottomless baskets of adorable bottles. He would have come into the city by now, just to ransack the Carlyle. But would he sit on the park benches? Because some of us would not sit on them. Could the *benches* kill you? A lifetime of feeling superior to anyone who couldn't hack the unpredictability of this town and now you're only as comfortable as the most cautious person in the room.

I went places the way swimmers kick themselves off a pool wall. Sometimes I was too exhausted by the prospect. There was a playground in Tribeca I avoided passing because I found the "S.S. Fun" stenciled on the seesaw to be a little much. Maybe the city was like Bettie Page, who wouldn't allow herself to be photographed after a certain age. We should avert our gaze out of respect. One evening, a barefoot woman followed me around my neighborhood, screaming, "HELLO! HELLO! CAN YOU TREAT ME LIKE A REGULAR HUMAN BEING?!" The more I ignored her, the louder she screamed: "CAN YOU JUST TREAT ME LIKE A REGULAR HUMAN BEING?! LIKE YOU WOULD ANY REGULAR HUMAN BEING?!" When we arrived at an avenue, I turned around and roared: "I AM!"

The whole planet had taken on an unfamiliar shape. Lights out in the City of Lights, game over in Sin City. Still, we were being watched. Maybe because we'd spent the better part of a century forcing the rest of the world to watch us. They'd seen the dystopian movies: First, New Yorkers can't get off the island. Next, they sneak into Radio City Music Hall and have sex onstage. Then they eat one another. So, for God's sake, act accordingly. We wanted outsiders to appreciate how bad it was to live in close quarters with so much inescapable hardship. The miracle of life in New York has never been survival but experience, the individual stories that meld into a collective one. We *wanted* others to be horrified by this damage to our essence, to be agog at the tents springing up in bike lanes, Times Square drained to *Vanilla Sky* levels, the Empire State Building blinking red like a heartbeat (or an SOS), while simultaneously telegraphing that *no!* Only *we* were allowed to be scared. New York isn't "over," you fair-weather friends. Go be drama queens on someone else's television. Stop staring. Send flowers.

At least I felt granted permission to let the depression curl up and sleep next to me. I'd dedicated so much time to negotiating with loss, time everyone assumed I was using for what the fitness instructors call "active recovery." At least now I didn't feel out of step with the mood of the city. That's right, everyone get on my level. Everyone eye the showerhead with contempt. In Kay Redfield Jamison's seminal book on suicide, *Night Falls Fast,* for which Russell was the publicist, she writes: "The horror of profound depression, and the hopelessness that usually accompanies it, are hard to imagine for those who have not experienced them. Because the despair is private, it is resistant to clear and compelling description." Depression will always be a challenge to illustrate—it's woefully plotless, "a storm of murk," as William Styron dubbed it—but a mass depressive event has a leg up on this truth.

In Manhattan, we had box seats to the blood draining out. The retaining walls of Xanadu were in our backyard. The depeopled Strawberry Fields and the rows of police cars double-parked outside the UN (was now a good time for a terrorist attack?). The sound of subway announcements, drifting up through the grates. The stations themselves started to look fake, like a model of a town. For the first time, I thought of Manhattan as an island. I'd always known. Its geological status was not a secret. How did I think I got here? But as I paced its edges, my inability to dive into the water and swim away was thrown into sharp relief. The famous buildings seemed almost organic. They jutted up from the ground yet served no purpose, the way a boulder might take on the import of the Chrysler Building on a deserted island. Someone had *built* the Chrysler Building. That ballerina of our skyline, our proof of good taste. How deranged. Someone had designed it, gathered materials, and decided: This will go here. People will go inside it. And the question now is why and what for?

Years ago, I became obsessed with the idea of writing an article on lucid dreaming. I liked the notion that one could make a lemonade stand appear in the middle of a bad dream, even if I didn't believe it was possible. My pitch was universally rejected. Apparently, "people dream" is not a news hook. But while searching for an angle, I called up the world's foremost expert on the matter, a professor at Stanford, and asked his assistant some preliminary questions. Most journalists considered lucid dreaming to be a pseudoscience, and this assistant had had it up to *here* with fielding calls from skeptics like me. I didn't make it past the gate. But I will never forget how casually she referred to reality as "waking life." Not "consciousness" or "daytime" or plain "life," but a state on par with dreaming. I thought about that conversation a lot during those first weeks of spring, when the only thing that made my life a life was that I was awake for it.

Russell and I were alike in that our attachment to where we were from was tenuous, having been sacrificed on the altar of urban allegiance. Russell sloughed off his hometown on purpose, came

164 | SLOANE CROSLEY

to New York as one of the city's queer refugees. I sloughed off mine because it's what I'd been trained to do as a suburban kid—to look at New York, to hope for New York, to feel defined by and inferior to New York. The math was different but the conclusion was the same. It's not that there are wrong reasons to come to New York (though there are plenty of questionable desertion polemics), but in reality-show parlance? Russell was here for the right reasons. He came for the carnival, his collection of *Playbills* piled alongside the books. A sample of his cultural intake in the months before he died: Two dance performances, four films, productions of *Porgy and Bess, Merrily We Roll Along, La Traviata, Ain't Too Proud: The Life and Times of the Temptations, High Button Shoes, Hadestown, Burn This, Lady in the Dark, White Noise* at the Public Theater, Handel's *Messiah* at Carnegie Hall, and *Call Me Madam* at City Center ("Pretty good, even without Ethel Merman"). This is someone who attended a book event a week for twenty years.

"We tell ourselves stories in order to live . . ." So begins the embraced-to-the-point-of-asphyxiation Didion passage from *The White Album*. The line continues with: "We look for the sermon in the suicide." If there is a sermon to be found in what happened to Russell, it's that he needed to be *told* stories in order to live. He approached his life through the lens of fiction. It was how he divided the world into villains and victims, how he diagnosed those closest to him, how he diagnosed himself. He was not the first gay man in New York with an affinity for performance, but his addiction served not as a supplement to life, but, too often, as replacement for a story of his own. It was his way of weaseling out of the arduous task of recognizing his own gray areas, by framing everything through *Carmen* or *Tosca*. To wit: He was never big on museums. All the humanity, none of the humans. Call him when the paintings start sleeping with each other.

Once, I took him to a seedy bar near the Port Authority Bus Terminal with a secret passageway to a marginally less seedy bar. He spied an empty cocaine vial on the floor, grabbed my hand, and rotated my rings around. I told him he was being ridiculous.

"Am I?!" he asked.

But when we popped out into the second bar, Russell's face lit up. They were having a "roaring twenties" night.

"It's like *The Skin of Our Teeth* in here!" he announced.

I saw my first opera with Russell, at the age of twenty-six, when he took me to *La Bohème*. *La Bohème* has a Dear Hustler setup that's easy to follow. Four starving artists distract their landlord from their overdue rent by taking him out of town. But one stays behind. Suddenly, there's a knock at his door. Why, it's the cute seamstress down the hall who needs a light for her candle. Thus begins their doomed romance (she has consumption, he dumps her, they get back together, she dies anyway).

During the performance, I obsessively consulted the subtitles on the panel in front of me. *La Bohème* may be straightforward, but it also features a character that plays the violin for a rich man's parrot. This is not something I would've picked up on in Italian.

Russell kept moving his hand over my screen and shaking his head.

"You can watch TV at home," he whispered.

"I'm not watching TV," I said, brushing his hand away. "I'm reading."

"You can read at home."

Then he pointed at the stage and said, in his best *Soylent Green*:

"People! It's people!"

The movies go so far as to glamorize a New York without people. All those sneaky tours of the Metropolitan Museum and Yankee Stadium. Soak it in, rookie. Your future is bright. Some moments shared this tenor: Would you like your own subway car? Your chariot awaits. How about this unobstructed view of anything? Now wave at that hawk, perched on a stop sign. But any moment longer than this turned sour. One of Russell's favorite quotes was "I'd rather cry in the back of a Rolls-Royce than be happy on a bicycle," which he insisted on misattributing to Elizabeth Taylor (it's Patrizia Reggiani, ex-wife of Maurizio Gucci, who had her husband murdered). But now the quote had nowhere to land. What would anyone do with a Rolls-Royce in Manhattan but sell it or sit in the street and lean on the horn?

I did not feel *pampered* by the sparseness of New York. I felt a menacing inertia, like my life had become petrified in ash. And because the entire city felt the same way, there was no way out. In Freud's seminal essay on loss, "Mourning and Melancholia," he writes, "When melancholia occurs where we would expect mourning, we suspect a pathological position, but, generally, we don't consider mourning pathological, we expect it to be overcome after a lapse of time." Because we did not know when the pandemic would end, only that it would get worse, the depression did not feel like something to surmount or snap out of; it felt Sisyphean.

This feeling was at odds with the chaotic visual and cinematic history of New York. The backdrop of the city remains even when the players do not. We have all those concrete stages that hosted *The Warriors, Do the Right Thing, West Side Story, Midnight Cowboy, Shaft*, Michael J. Fox cowering in a phone booth, Bob Dylan on Jones Street, the Beastie Boys on Rivington, Nan Goldin at Stonewall, Jane Fonda and Donald Sutherland outside Central Park, Alfred Stieglitz in Midtown, Audrey Hepburn's bejeweled walk of shame, Jason Alexander pushing a Frogger console through traffic, Chloë Sevigny kicking a dog on the Upper East Side, Griffin Dunne sprinting through Soho, *Wild Style* in the Bronx, Eddie Murphy on Wall Street, Madonna outside Love Saves the Day, Andy Warhol and Edie Sedgwick bursting out of a manhole on Fifty-eighth Street, Al Pacino in Needle Park, Al Pacino outside the St. Regis, Al Pacino on Minetta Street, Al Pacino in Tudor City, Al Pacino screaming "Attica!" To be depressed among these stories is a reminder that you are not retreating from the world, you got left by it.

Instead of sleeping, I did things like jog up the spine of Fifth Avenue at dawn, where I didn't see a single car. While planning Russell's memorial service, I'd fantasized about shutting down Fifth Avenue for one hour. *One.* Not all of them. Even if I had seen a car, we'd gotten in the habit of moseying out of their way at our own pace. For their part, the cars remained alert. A consensus had been reached: We weren't living through this shit only to get mowed over in a crosswalk. I spun in the street but, unable to reach the dissociative heights necessary to forget the circumstances that brought me here, I wound up cackling at my reflection in storefronts. How many minutes until these windows hosted another reflection? How long until my earrings hurt when I pushed them back in? What was stopping me from shaving one leg only? I may not have had a partner, but I could grow a crop of anything.

Sometimes I was lonely, sometimes I was just alone. This is the kind of distinction people make after breakups, as if loneliness is what happens to you when you fail to be alone. These states flickered on and off when I was between relationships, sometimes taking the form of bolts of pain, sometimes of dullness itself as I moved forward, content to know a wise choice had been made by at least one party. But the lingo of self-empowerment felt out of place, compounded by fantasies about the past: What would it have been like to have someone help me scrub fingerprint dust from my floorboards the night of the burglary? Or a hand on my back as I cried about Russell until my jaw ached? If Russell had never died, I might be up in Connecticut, listening to him pace outside my room until I emerged.

The anxiety may have been a blanket but the sadness was a knife.

Sometimes I imagined a folded universe in which the pandemic and the burglary overlapped. The burglary wouldn't have happened. It just wouldn't have. I barely left my apartment, which was conducive to some types of theft (packages were stolen with such regularity, calling UPS became part of the delivery process) but prohibitive to home invasions. On the police report, wedged between the "date of occurrence" box and the "domestic relationship" box, there was a box entitled "name of gang."

How would that work now? A socially distanced gang?

But there was never going to *be* a version of the story in which it wasn't my missing jewelry and my dead friend. You can ignore grief. You push it around your plate. But you can't give it away.

One night, around 3:00 a.m., I searched for Russell's name in my phone. I thought I could revisit our texts without too much psychological damage. I'd done the same thing of late, watching YouTube clips of him when he was younger, standing behind podiums, introducing authors. You can tell how unnatural it is for him to be so formal and yet how much he delights in the company of those worthy enough to film. Or I'd play one of the videos I had of the two of us standing outside a leather bar in Chelsea, him refusing to take me inside. I found his voice to be a comfort. I should've left it at the videos.

I scrolled until I was looking at texts from 2018. That summer, there were several high-profile New York suicides. Kate Spade hanged herself in her apartment. Three days later, Anthony Bourdain died the same way while staying at a hotel in France. The year before that, Jean Stein, author of Russell's beloved *Edie*, jumped from her fifteenth-floor penthouse on the Upper East Side. You would think the warm weather would see a decrease in suicides but it's the reverse. Scientists have speculated about biochemical shifts or factors like increased access to the outdoors, but surely we don't need the scientists for this. The mood differential is too great. It's smelling lilacs through a mask that you can never take off.

And then I hit Jeanine. On June 17, 2018, Jeanine Pepler

hanged herself in her home. Jeanine was not famous. She was one of us, a publicist, except freelance, which meant a wider variety of projects. She represented vodka brands as well as books. We worked closely with her for a few months in 2004 because it was the twentieth anniversary of *Bright Lights, Big City* and Jay McInerney was one of her clients. The three of us planned a party at the Odeon. Jeanine made sure the invitations didn't look as if they'd come off a photocopier in a publishing house. The party overlapped with Halloween weekend, which explains why she commissioned a giant pumpkin to be carved with the novel's cover image, the twin towers lit up from the inside.

Page Six ran the news of her death. I texted Russell, who called right away, but I was on a plane, about to take off. So he tried a different medium:

I saw, he wrote.

So awful, I wrote.

Well death is so final.

I was leaving town for the weekend because I'd just been through a breakup, and while I no longer had a boyfriend, I did have a nonrefundable deposit at a hotel in Miami. When I landed, I was greeted with two new messages from Russell:

Let's make a deal: No killing yourself without my approval first. I'll do the same.

Let's make a deal: No killing yourself without my approval first. I'll do the same.

I flinched at the repetition before realizing this was a side effect of cellular networks catching up with themselves.

Done, I wrote, *but lol at the idea that you WOULD give your approval.*

I'd need to hear your argument in favor first. I'd be fair.
I'll have to live just to spite you.
Right back at you. Guess we're both going to live forever.
I threw my phone out of the room.

Grand Central remained open during the pandemic, it had to. So, when it got light out, I decided to pay a visit. As much as we loathed the sight of our own ceilings, we were lacking in them otherwise. This, too, contributed to the desert island feeling of New York: You've got your mud hut, maybe one other mud hut, and then outside. I wanted to see not just someone else's ceiling, but *the* ceiling.

I passed beneath the gargantuan American flag as I moved down the echoing slope to the main concourse. A man with a push broom wasn't gathering much in the way of debris. There were a few stragglers, including a woman in a turban, bolting for a train. After months of seeing people jog only for their health, it was peculiar to see someone *run*. But where to? It was 6:45 a.m. None of us had anywhere to be. That was the whole premise. She was wearing a dress, a cross-body bag wagging behind her. Moses in heels, she split the air. I thought of the scene from *Eternal Sunshine of the Spotless Mind* in which Jim Carrey and Kate Winslet race though the terminal as people disappear around them. Poof. Poof. Poof.

The brass dispensers at the information booth were still stocked with paper schedules. I slid a blue one out from the pack. The options seemed from another century. Still, I found myself registering a track number and floating beneath one of the archways, stepping through one of the half-open train doors and tucking myself in near the window. On the partition was an ad for a mattress company, guaranteeing the best sleep of my life.

I began filling the empty train seats with people. The woman who ran my dry cleaner's before the pandemic forced her to close up shop. I put her across from me, holding her prized photograph of her and Woody Allen on her lap. Woody Allen has never lived in my neighborhood. What he was doing at my dry cleaner's is beyond me. Behind her, I sat a cellist I knew in my early twenties when he was in his fifties. He invited me to the symphony and at intermission talked about his divorce. We never spoke again. Next to him, I put the guy I met at Lit Lounge. He complimented my sweater and speculated that I "didn't date Black dudes." When I asked him if this was his way of hitting on me, he said, "Obviously not." Next to him, I put the detective, my old friend, who was preoccupied with his necktie. In front of me, I put a woman with whom I'd had a run-in at the YMCA in my twenties. She accused me of cutting her in line for a treadmill. When I apologized, she whipped around and said, "Get the hell away from me, you probably cheat on tests!" It's a bittersweet thing, to be accused of being a bad person while also being confused for a college student.

Eventually, there was only one seat left.

It had been months since I'd felt Russell's presence, like I could talk to him. But now I could feel him by my side, down to the smell of his leather messenger bag.

"Hi," I whispered.

He smiled, which I took as an invitation to speak. I told him the city wasn't the same without him, which was true but only by coincidence. This seemed to confuse him. So I turned my whole body to face him, tucking up my knee.

"Okay, so something bad has happened . . ."

I told him about how I'd tried thinking of him as one dead snowflake in the blizzard that had blanketed the earth, a blizzard that had now begun to fall on the city too. I told him how I'd tried to mix his death in with the others to make it hurt less. Or hurt differently. Like feeding a dog its medicine in peanut butter. Except I was the dog. He grinned but didn't speak.

"You wouldn't have survived this, would you?"

He shook his head.

"You were so unhappy."

He nodded but didn't speak.

"Why didn't you tell me?"

He sighed, like after all this time, I should know better than to ask.

"I'm tired," I said, resting my temple on his shoulder.

Maybe the insomnia had been doing me a favor. Because whenever I did manage to pass out, in the form of an afternoon nap, I had a recurring nightmare. Each time, a different person I loved killed themselves. Each time, I spent the duration of the dream trying to prevent it. But I could never get there in time. Urban legend has it that if you die in your dreams, you die in "waking life" too. There's nothing in the bylaws about other people dying.

"What would make you happy?" I asked. "Do you want to go home?"

If you stayed on this train for several hours, past the hospital where I was born; past the Bronx, where my nice grandmother used to live; past Scarsdale, where my mean grandmother used to live; past White Plains, where my parents still live; past Mount Pleasant, where the cemetery runs up to the track; to the very last stop, you'd find yourself at a slip of a station near the Connecticut border. This is where Russell and his partner used to pick me up. There's an abandoned insane asylum across from the platform. It was once New York State's preeminent institution for frontal lobotomies.

Russell shook his head. He looked around the train. I looked with him.

He wanted people.

"Oh. Okay."

So I made a story for us. I staged an opera with words I couldn't understand but he could. I imagined the dramas between the actors. Maybe the fifty-year-old divorcé convinces the woman at the gym he's ready to be in a relationship but he's on the rebound and breaks her heart. Maybe the dry cleaner discovers something she shouldn't in a blazer pocket, something incriminating, and calls the detective, who frames the guy at Lit Lounge because, even in fantasy, he's a terrible detective. I imagined the swooning, the formidable cleavage, the ridiculous weeping.

The opera was interrupted by the sound of a bell. The train across the tracks shut its doors, lumbered forward, and disappeared. When I looked around again, everyone had vanished except for Russell, who was standing, flinging his bag over his shoulder.

"Don't go," I said. "You're dead. Where do you need to be in such a hurry?"

He leaned down and kissed my hand, flipping it back and forth. He was looking for the green dome ring.

"That I can't help you with. Believe me, I tried."

He frowned, sticking out his bottom lip.

"I have this, though."

Around my neck was a locket I'd bought myself over Christmas. My photograph selections were limited—it had to be a physical print of Russell's head and it had to fit. I did not relish the serial killer undertones of the cutting process, snipping where I had to snip. That spring, I carted it around as if it had a camera hidden inside. I'd angle it toward the things I wanted him to see. *Look at these trees in bloom! Look how beautiful!* I'd turned him into jewelry and jewelry into him. He seemed unimpressed.

"Hey, can I ask you something?"

He shrugged.

"Am I dreaming? I know it's dumb to ask, but I feel like you would know."

He didn't speak.

He turned and walked off the train, waving over his shoulder with one hand.

Thoughts drifted in and out in waves. I imagined taking this train home. I could go now. Home has never been a sanctuary for me. The house is compact, the relationships therein complicated. But I could surprise my parents with breakfast on the porch, where my mother, despite not having seen me in months, would complain of not having any makeup on. Sharing a cab with a stranger during a pandemic would not be ideal, but I could always walk from the station. It would take one hour. I'd done it once, as a teenager, when I'd lost my wallet. I was fighting with my father and refused to call to be picked up. This felt like a dicey proposition at the time, but it became not dicey quickly. It became a landscape of dentists' offices and delis, of churches and split-levels and Little League fields.

When you move to New York from the suburbs of New York, you don't leave home, you wake up one day having left. This transfer probably seems enviably seamless to those who grow up knowing the city from the outside, but the lack of delineation catches up with us eventually. We must choose to make this our story. We must recite the pledges, in sickness and in health, till death or Hollywood do us part. We must decide the city is worth its trials. It's a process most of our friends and neighbors, who had to pack up their whole lives in order to be here, went through years ago. This moment is unheralded, but when it's done, a transformation happens. Where we are from and where we call home can, at long last, pull apart. Like repotting plants. We become not just resigned to, but full of pride for the city's endless parade of handicaps, for the ordeals that shape us. For the family it gave us. For the family it took away.

A conductor knocked on the ceiling to get my attention. I sat up, disoriented but awake.

"Miss," he said—Miss! God bless these masks!—"this train won't leave for an hour. Are you staying or going?"

And I stood.

PART V
THE VERTICAL EARTH

(AFTERWARD)

Years later, I will be at a party in Los Angeles, a party you'd hate, when a woman will start playing with the locket. I don't mind. People touch each other's jewelry. It's a form of intimacy. The way we pop an earlobe toward us or tug at someone else's fingers—these gestures expose the dormant thief in all of us. A locket is a unique kind of invitation, sharing more DNA with a tattoo than a necklace. But suddenly, I will hear this woman say: "And who's this little guy?" I will look down and be stunned stupid. She has opened the locket. With my neck on a short leash, she is examining her discovery.

I have not laid eyes on this version of your face since I cut your head off with a pair of kitchen scissors. Your hair is closely cropped, your jaw more defined than I remember. I tell the woman the truth: You are my friend and you died. Information I would've gladly offered up without the interactive portion of this conversation. The temptation to say more, to use your suicide to teach her a lesson in etiquette, is strong: Don't ask questions you don't want to know the answers to. Don't go around touching other people's hair or their pregnant bellies or opening up other people's lockets. What if you had fallen out? I feign a distraction and get myself to a bathroom mirror.

Are you okay? Yes, you are okay. You are fine. Everything is fine.

In the photograph, you are forty-four. My age.

It's starting. I am catching up with you.

Looking you in the eye for the first time in so long, I think there's one last thing you should know. Something from the beginning. Maybe you know it already.

August 27, 2019. A Tuesday. The Amazon is on fire. The world is not yet masked. People are milling about my neighborhood, grousing into their phones, making their evening plans. I am sitting on the stoop, talking to you in my head: *You've put a permanent damper on my birthday, pulling a stunt like this the same week. How could you?* I smile and drag my fingers down my face. *What am I going to do without you?*

Inside the restaurant, they have prematurely framed the windows with little white lights. There's a bald man in your chair, laughing between bites. You've been gone for a mere month and yet I already feel like I'm wallowing. This is a naïve thought process, a real misreading of the size of the map. I don't yet realize that it unfolds. All I know is I want to get as far away as I can from the weight of this sorrow. From telling the story of how you died and getting it all wrong. I am not ready to accept anything, to face anyone. Perhaps this is why I decide that I need, as I have never needed anything in my life, to jump off a cliff.

And not just any cliff. I have one in mind.

Tucked away on Sydney's eastern shores, there's a wall of rock that juts out thirty-six feet above the harbor. It's hard to wrap one's mind around what thirty-six vertical feet looks like from above, exactly, but if one were to drop a book into the water, it would take a moment to spot it again. The cliff is not advertised in guidebooks. It's accessible by hiking through some woods, hopping a fence, and poking around until one spots a warning sign the size of a cheese board. Physics being more of a suggestion than a hard-and-fast rule for Australians, the sign features a single line of text: SERIOUS INJURIES HAVE OCCURRED IN PERSONS JUMPING FROM THIS CLIFF. Does injury occur within a person or to a person? Well, if that isn't the question of the hour.

I am familiar with the cliff because, a decade ago, I tried, and failed, to jump off it. I was invited to the same literary festival in Melbourne, and since I was not about to fly to Australia for a weekend, I tacked on Sydney.

When you came over to my apartment the last night I saw you, you couldn't understand why I'd go *back* to Australia if I didn't absolutely have to. It was such a hassle, only to land myself in a place that wasn't different enough from America. It was not, to use your word, "France." I shrugged. To be summoned is exciting. You lived your life surrounded by authors whose novels were covered with foil awards stickers when they weren't being burned. The whole world played tug-of-war with their time. But the only other city to which I'd ever been flown, paid, and immortalized via promotional poster was Wichita Falls, Texas. Wichita Falls is home to "the world's littlest skyscraper." It's forty feet high. So, I guess imagine trying, and failing, to jump off a very small skyscraper.

Ask me again. Ask me again, now that you are dead, why I'd go back to Australia if I could get out of it, precisely *because* you are dead. Part of me has the same thought process I had when I was told you'd killed yourself (that's how your partner said it, semantics were not his priority): If I follow the plan, maybe nothing will be wrong. But really, it's because I think this trip will, paradoxically, bring me closer to you.

When the cops were milling around my living room the night of the burglary, I kept having to remind myself that I'd invited them. Answering inane questions during those vital hours was like being asked to recite a fairy tale in the middle of a car chase. *No, I don't know how long I've lived here, and yes, I might be off by a year. Shall we drop everything while I find my lease?* I had the sharpest sense that these people were *in my way.* The only people that counted were me and the thief. It was borderline romantic: A marriage sealed in carbon, a runaway groom. It's the same with you. It doesn't matter how others have come to know about your suicide, doesn't matter if I have told them myself, I can't seem to find a moment alone with you. It's the sensation of being in a crowd, angling to see a famous painting. This crowd consists of people you know but also of people you don't know. I don't know them either. But they're out there. Every day, new people are being reminded of how they are connected to you, of when they might have been in the same room, of where they might have seen your name. They are searching in their in-boxes, assessing their nearness to tragedy and moving on.

I need to get as far away from them as possible, to a place where no new people can bloom. A place free of associations, where you yourself have never set foot. And when I get there, I need to peer into an abyss. To see something of what you saw.

Given my shaky mental state in August 2019, friends express concern when I tell them I'm thinking of jumping off a cliff.

I don't mean to shock them. Nothing about this time period requires extra narrative flair. I only mean to experiment with a little gallows humor (ha!) in the mode of "enough rope to hang yourself" (ha!). I try reassuring them with backstory: During that first trip to Sydney, I was sitting alone at a bar, reading a book, when I was befriended by a woman named Bec. Bec grew up in rural Queensland. One of her earliest memories is of discovering a frill-necked lizard pacing in her bathtub. She fears not the great outdoors. One summer, after college, after she'd moved to Sydney, Bec and her friends stumbled upon the cliff and dared one another to jump. As she told me this, I put away my book and thought: I should definitely make this woman take me to a ledge and push me off it. After all, why are we on this planet if not to bring ourselves to its edges?

These are the kinds of batshit questions Australia invites you to ask.

The following morning, the two of us stood stock-still, like gargoyles, the wind whipping off the gray harbor in ornery gales.

During the winter, you can propel yourself into this liquid stucco only at high tide, but at high tide there's no way to gauge the topography of the rocks. Also, shooting straight into the harbor from that height is a free enema. Also, the cliff is located in a section of the harbor called, not for nothing, Shark Bay. In the end, neither of us jumped. We drove to the Park Hyatt, sat in the lobby in our dry wetsuits, and ordered martinis.

Somehow, this story alleviates no one's concerns.

So I start lying. I should not be jumping off cliffs. Agreed. Jumping will not knock out the time I didn't jump. Nor will it bring you back. It's also a potentially humiliating way to die. I will go to Melbourne and come straight home. We have a memorial to plan and it's not mine.

I book a sixty-dollar flight to Sydney and tell no one.

Actually, I tell one person.

She texts back: *Your wetsuit is still hanging in my garage.*

If I felt in the summer of 2019 how I feel now, I would not have gone back to Sydney. This is not because I was crazy in 2019 and now am not crazy. I don't think I was particularly insane then, nor do I find myself particularly sane now. Those who think of me as healed are not looking carefully enough and those who thought of me as certifiable were not looking carefully enough. Though who wouldn't be grateful to be thought of at all? "There is only one liberty," wrote Camus, "to come to terms with death. After which, everything is possible." By now, I have come to terms. Rather, your suicide has brought the terms to me. *Your suicide*. As if it belongs to you. As if you rescued it from the flea market. *Your suicide.* A manner of death so frightening, we give it back to the dead as soon as it happens, unhanding it like hot coal.

But I still miss you like you wouldn't believe. The years have done nothing to dull the missing. Remember that time an author gave us acupuncture sessions? Yours passed without incident, but I didn't realize how still I was meant to stay. I turned my head halfway through. It felt like being punched in the spine.

"It's just pain leaving the body," the acupuncturist said. "You don't have to hold on to it. It's already happened."

My neck hurt for a week.

This is how your death is. A constant ache. It's such effort to avoid attaching every disappointment to you, to stop punishing others for not being you, to stop treating your suicide as a freak accident, robbing you of control when I only wanted to relieve you of blame. How do I keep you buried and keep you with me at the same time? This is the biggest riddle of them all.

When the existence of this book is announced on social media, strangers respond, saying they are sorry for my loss. I am desperate to ask them: So, you agree, then? You agree he's dead? Why would you share this broken heart emoji if he were not dead? How come you get to know, instantly, what took me all these words to know? I find I cannot have an interaction with a new person, a person you would have adored, without wondering if I am meeting the friend you needed. Is this the person for whom you would have lived just a little longer? Is this the person who would have shown you how to keep going? What if I was the wrong friend for you? What if we were all the wrong people for you?

―――――――

Bec comes running out of her house, barefoot, to greet me. I tell her she looks exactly the same and she returns the compliment. In her case, it's true in a way that extends beyond hydration. Bec is a youthful person, the kind who makes fast friends of transient Americans. Two children and ten years later, she says she is still game to jump.

Her husband is away for the evening so I take his side of the bed. As I get ready for our sleepover, digging in my bag for face wash, her four-year-old son pads into the bedroom wearing footed pajamas. He has something to tell me and I am to listen very carefully. I pull up a chair. He informs me that I am, under no circumstances, to wet the bed. Because even if I wet only *part* of the bed, "they will still have to change all the sheets." He rolls his eyes, as if we both know how unreasonable adults can be. Then he runs down the hall to his mother, who is beckoning him to come brush his teeth. I watch as she ushers him into the bathroom.

"What?" she asks.

"Nothing," I say, smiling.

There is no way she's jumping.

I've been pacing for an hour, me in my wetsuit and Bec in her shore-bound jeans and cardigan. It has been decided, over a breakfast of Cheerios, that *someone* has to keep watch. *Someone* has to be able to run for help just in case. I agree, these are excellent points. But now, perhaps because she's wearing the associated gear, her motherly concern transfers to me. She decides the water is looking "a bit sharky." I reject this, pointing out that there's a Diamond Bay around here somewhere and it's not like it's *lined with diamonds*. She frowns. The aerial view of seagulls is not helping. The horizon is streaked with ominous clouds that seem to emanate from the skyline like rays. The wind is force-feeding me my own hair.

I kick off my sneakers and whip my coat into a tree. I instruct Bec to count to ten. She holds up her phone to film the occasion. At first, I think I will surprise her and jump at six. Or eight. But then I shake my wrists and jog in place and make her start again from the top. I stop short of the edge each time. There's a term for this type of activity: suicide drills. I want nothing more than to spring off this cliff. I have bent over backward to make it possible. But I cannot. It's not that I am afraid, although I am most definitely that, it's that my muscles freeze when they get close to the edge. My brain has decided this looks an awful lot like death. I try to trick it. *It's not so bad. Just pretend you're being chased. Pretend your feet are being scorched by lava.* But my body isn't buying it.

I spray the air with epithets and plop down in defeat. Bec tells me it's okay, an excuse for me to come back in the summer, when the petrifaction has been reduced by a factor of ten. Okay, I say, sure. Perhaps Bec and I will see each other again in this life, perhaps not. If you were alive, there would be no chance of you crossing paths with her. Zero. Why is that? How come you didn't see the great wheel of the world and find a different spoke? Were you so jaded and impatient? Weren't you curious about what would happen tomorrow and the day after that? This is a juvenile reaction to suicide. I've mostly avoided it. But why *didn't* you just clear out your bank account, go somewhere, and reevaluate? Or make a whole new life before vowing to end it, like Gauguin? You could have run away from an existence that felt small to one that felt big. You'd done it before.

In the story "Paul's Case," by Willa Cather, a story you loved, an alienated boy flees his hometown and escapes to New York, intent on having his first—and last—hurrah. But he senses his own limits:

> He reflected drowsily, to the swell of the music and the chill sweetness of his wine, that he might have done it more wisely. He might have caught an outbound steamer and been well out of their clutches before now. But the other side of the world had seemed too far away and too uncertain then; he could not have waited for it; his need had been too sharp. If he had to choose over again, he would do the same thing tomorrow.

In the end, Paul jumps in front of a train.

Bec needs to make a call and says she'll meet me at the car. After she disappears into the woods, I think: *Here we are, alone at last, on the other side of the world.* I am embarrassed to articulate such fantastical thinking, but I'm not here just to get closer to you: I'm here to get closer to *finding* you.

I am in still in the early stages of grieving and I find it suspicious that you are not lurking around this planet *somewhere.* I have been making silent vows to find you: If you are in the trees, I will climb them. If you are in the bushes, I will trim them. If you are in the ocean, I will drain it. *Every day is an opportunity to confirm where the necklace is not.* So why not here? Why not some place where you thought no one would come looking for you?

But when I crawl to the cliff's edge and let my head hang down over the abyss, there is nothing. I focus on the folded napkin of the opera house to keep myself from getting dizzy. There's no sign of you. There is only the wind and the inky waves, rising and falling to their own tempo. Even the seagulls have gone.

You leaped into a noose. A NOOSE.

Are you out of your fucking mind?

You must have jumped at two. I know you and I know that's what you did.

My temples are starting to tingle so I roll over, stand up, and unzip my wetsuit pocket. Inside is half a gold chain. It's the chain that snapped in two when the thief ripped the egg shelves out of the cabinet. It's all that was left that night. I have put it in a plastic sandwich bag and brought it with me. As I hold it up, I hear a magpie in a tree behind me, squawking, adjusting its white cape. I tell it to back off. If any part of you is in the jewelry, then it feels right to throw you over the edge. To decide that this is where you are, even if you are not, even if I never visit you again. To give just one thing up voluntarily.

Months later, I am moving a bookshelf in my bedroom, wiggling it away from the wall to clean an already-pristine patch of floor. The pandemic has coaxed out the obsessive-compulsive in us all. Moving the furniture for no reason used to be the purview of upstairs neighbors the world over. Now it's a Sunday afternoon.

In doing this, I get a fresh view of my books. The deckled ones have collected dust. I'm not even sure where they got ahold of dust. Then I see something shiny wedged in the belly of one of the books.

I pinch and pull, bringing it close to my face. I am already on the floor but sit, somehow, more on the floor. This is the other half of the gold chain. It has been here all along. And now its other half is ten thousand miles away, at the bottom of the ocean.

I push down on the clasp, making it talk.

The book is *Edie*.

There is a park in Kassel, Germany, a midsized city home to an installation by the artist Walter de Maria called *The Vertical Earth Kilometer*, which has to be the most easily overlooked public art in history. It passes for a coin in the middle of a dirt path, so much so that one is tempted to pick it up. But one would not have much luck. The coin is actually the end of a brass rod that shoots straight into the ground for almost a mile. For years, both before and after I saw *The Vertical Earth Kilometer* in person, I assumed a considerable part of the rod's appeal had to do with a diametrically oppositional rod. An antipode.

I have no idea where I got this idea. This alleged counterpart would have to be in the middle of the South Pacific. It would take a little more than an artist's grant and some scuba gear to install it. Even if it were possible for such a thing to exist, this was never the point, to put the world on a spit. *The Vertical Earth Kilometer* reaches down, unanswered. It also gets stepped on all day long. Now I have my own version of *The Vertical Earth Kilometer*.

Except my object did get split in two. My object does cry out for its other half. From every Jewish wedding: May your marriage last as long as it would take to reassemble this glass.

It turns out that most things don't end too many times, Russell. Most things don't end at all. So much is still unsolved. I still want to know where everything I loved has gone and why. Perhaps if I knew more about God, I would know it's blasphemous to want answers, and perhaps if I knew more about philosophy, I would know it's foolish to suggest there are answers. Maybe one day, in a world that looks reasonably enough like this one, you'll tell me. But for now, I must poke holes in all this curiosity so that I might breathe, so that I might get on with the second half of my life. If I desire the kind of life you wanted me to live, one of expansion over retraction, I must learn to be on the side of the living.

I must learn to accept that we are not the same.

My grief for you will always remain unruly, even as I know it contains the logic of everyone who has ever felt it. Sometimes I close my eyes so that I can listen to it spread. So that I can *make* it spread. I run it up the walls of my apartment. I listen to it circle the doorframes and propel itself out the window. I can hear it clonking down the fire escape, cracking the concrete as it lands. Sometimes I hear it in the rivers, sloshing against the stone, or in the subway screeching to a halt. And then, because I cannot call you home, I call it home. I open my eyes and in a flash it comes back to me, zipping itself to my edges, bobbing between my fingers. It's made a real life for itself here. Oblivious to its own power, it snores so sweetly on my chest, this outline of a woman whose time has not yet come.

ACKNOWLEDGMENTS

Thank you to my agent, Jay Mandel, my editor, Sean McDonald, and the entire FSG team.

Russell once showed me a photograph of himself being chased by a friend's toddler. "Who is so awful?" he asked. "Who is beloved by children and animals?" I wish I had answered him: No one. No one is so awful.

This book is also in memory of Stephen McNabb.

If you or someone you know is struggling with suicidal thoughts, confidential assistance is available through the Suicide & Crisis Lifeline by calling or texting 988.

A Note About the Author

Sloane Crosley is the author of the novels *Cult Classic* and *The Clasp*, as well as three essay collections: *Look Alive Out There* and the *New York Times* bestsellers *I Was Told There'd Be Cake* and *How Did You Get This Number*. She lives in New York City.